Dictionary of Computing

Updated with the latest technologies

Windows – Networking – Help Desk – Social Media – Web Design

2015

Dictionary of Computing

Fully updated with the latest technologies 1.0

Windows – Networking – Help Desk – Social Media – Web Design

2015

All names mentioned on this book are the trademarks of their respective owners.

Tabla de contenido

Numbers and Symbols

*   1. A character used in applications and programming languages to signify multiplication. 2. In Windows, and other operating systems, a wildcard character that can be used in place of one or more characters, as in *.*, which represents any combination of a filename and an extension. 3. In the C and C++ programming languages, the character used to dereference a pointer to a class or structure.

..   Command Prompt and UNIX syntax for the parent directory. A single dot refers to the current directory.

/   1. A character used to separate parts of a directory path in UNIX and FTP or parts of an Internet address (URL) in Web browsers. 2. A character used to flag switches or parameters that control the execution of a program invoked through a command-line interface. See also command-line interface.

//   Notation used with a colon to separate the URL protocol (such as http or ftp) from the URL host machine name, as in http://www.facebook.com. See also URL.

/etc   The directory on UNIX in which most of the configuration information is kept. See Also UNIX.

/etc/passwd   The UNIX file that stores all of the account information, including username, password (encrypted form), the user identifier, the primary group the user belongs to, some additional information about the account (such as the real human name or other personal parameters), the user's home directory, and the login shell.This file is of particular interest to crackers; if they can read files from this directory, they can use the information to attack the machine. See Also Password; Shell; UNIX.

: Colon, a symbol used after the protocol name (such as http or ftp) in a URL. See also URL.

? In some operating systems and applications, a wildcard character often used to represent any other single character.

@ The separator between account names and domain names in Internet e-mail addresses. When spoken, @ is read as "at." Therefore, user@host.com would be read as "user at host dot com."

<>. 1. Angle brackets, a pair of symbols used to enclose a keyword, comprising a tag in an HTML, SGML, or XML document. See also HTML, SGML, XML. 2. A pair of symbols used to enclose a return address in an e-mail header.

>. Right angle bracket, a symbol used in some operating systems, such as Command Prompt and UNIX, to direct the output resulting from some command into a file. 2. A symbol commonly used in e-mail messages to designate text included from another message.

0-day. Zero Day or 0-day, in the security context, indicates that someone takes advantage of a security vulnerability on the same day when the vulnerability becomes generally known.

0G (Wireless). 0G refers to pre-cellular mobile telephony technology. These mobile telephones were usually mounted in cars or trucks. Typically, the transceiver (transmitter-receiver) is mounted in the vehicle trunk and attached to the "head" (dial, display, and handset) mounted near the driver seat.

0wn. A hacker culture term (typically spelled with a zero and not an O) meaning to control completely. For example, a system broken into by a hacker or cracker is under complete control of the perpetrator. See Also Crackers; Hacker.

100Base-T. An Ethernet standard for baseband LANs (local area networks) using twisted-pair cable carrying 100 Mbps (megabits per second). The 100Base-T standard is comprised of 100Base-T4 (four pairs of medium-grade to high-grade twisted-pair cable) and 100Base-TX (two pairs of high-grade twisted-pair cable). Also called: Fast Ethernet. See also Ethernet (definition 1).

10Base-T. The Ethernet standard for baseband LANs (local area networks) using twisted-pair cable carrying 10 Mbps (megabits per second) in a star topology. All nodes are connected to a central hub known as a multiport repeater. See also Ethernet (definition 1), star network, twisted-pair cable.

1394. See IEEE 1394, also FireWire port

16-bit application. An application written to run on a computer with a 16-bit architecture or operating system, such as MS-DOS or Windows 3.x.

16-bit color. Characteristic of a display that can produce 216 (65,536) distinct colors. Compare 24-bit color, 32-bit color.

16-bit machine. A computer that works with data in groups of 16 bits at a time. A computer may be considered a 16-bit machine either because its microprocessor operates internally on 16-bit words or because its data bus can transfer 16 bits at a time. The IBM PC/AT and similar models based on the Intel 80286 microprocessor are 16-bit machines in terms of both the word size of the microprocessor and the size of the data bus. The Apple Macintosh Plus and Macintosh SE use a microprocessor with a 32-bit word length (the Motorola 68000), but they have 16-bit data buses and are generally considered 16-bit machines.

16-bit operating system. An operating system, now outdated, that can work with 2 bytes, or 16 bits, of information at one time. A 16-bit operating system, such as MS-DOS and

Microsoft Windows 3.x, reflects the functionality of a 16-bit processor because the software and the chip must work together so closely. The main advantage of a 16-bit operating system over its earlier 8-bit predecessors (such as CP/M-80) was its ability to address more memory and use a larger (16-bit) bus. Sixteen-bit operating systems have since been eclipsed by 32-bit operating systems—such as the Macintosh operating system, Microsoft Windows NT, and Windows 9x—and by 64-bit operating systems, such as some versions of UNIX. See also 32-bit operating system.

1999 problem. 1. A variation on the Year 2000 problem in computer systems that have two-digit years in date fields and are used by companies and organizations in which the fiscal year 2000 begins before the end of calendar year 1999. These computer systems may interpret the fiscal year as the year 1900. 2. A potential problem, if not corrected, with date fields in older code that were (sometimes) used to hold values with special meaning. For example, the date 9/9/99 was often used as an expiration date meaning "keep this information forever" or, worse, "destroy this document immediately."

1G (Wireless). First Generation Wireless technology (1G) is the original analog, voice-only cellular telephone standard, developed in the 1980s. One such standard is NMT (Nordic Mobile Telephone), used in Nordic countries, Eastern Europe and Russia. Others include AMPS (Advanced Mobile Phone System) used in the United States, TACS (Total Access Communications System) in the United Kingdom, JTAGS in Japan, C-Netz in West Germany, Radiocom 2000 in France, and RTMI in Italy. Analog cellular service is being phased out in most places worldwide.

2068. This is the American version of the Spectrum. It has an additional 8K extension ROM, cartridge port, two joystick ports and AY-3-8912 sound chip with extra Sinclair BASIC commands to support these devices (STICK, SOUND). It was packaged in a hard plastic silver case with nonstandard plastic keys.

Image 1: TS 2068 computer

24-bit color. RGB color in which the level of each of the three primary colors in a pixel is represented by 8 bits of information. A 24-bit color image can contain over 16 million different colors. Not all computer monitors support 24-bit color, especially older models.

Those that do not may use 8-bit color (256 colors) or 16-bit color (65,536 colors). Also called: true color. See also bit depth, pixel, RGB. Compare 16-bit color, 32-bit color.

2600 Hz. The tone that long-distance companies such as American Telephone and Telegraph used to indicate that the long-distance lines were open. This knowledge was used by early-day phreaker John Draper (a.k.a. Cap'n Crunch) and is the lead-in title for 2600:The Hacker Quarterly, a popular computer underground magazine.

2G (Wireless). 2G stands for the second generation of mobile Wireless communication technology, which uses the digital technologies for the mobile communication. 2G technologies can be divided into TDMA-based (GSM) and CDMA-based standards depending on the type of multiplexing used. It allows slow data communications, but its primary focus is voice.

32:16. The Fortune 32:16 series of machines was intended to bridge the gap between the personal computer and the "mini" computer. The model we have is considered to be at the higher end of the offerings, with the entire system (including software) costing almost $30,000. The machine runs UNIX and is capable of controlling multiple terminals. The expansion system shown here adds a streaming tape backup to the unit.

Image 2: Fortune 32:16

32-bit application. An application written to run on a computer with a 32-bit architecture or operating system, such as Mac OS or Windows.

32-bit color. RGB color that is similar to 24-bit color, with 8 additional bits used to allow for faster transfer of an image"s color. See also bit depth, RGB. Compare 16-bit color, 24-bit color.

32-bit machine. A computer that works with data in groups of 32 bits at a time. The Apple Macintosh II and higher models are 32-bit machines, in terms of both the word size of their microprocessors and the size of the data buses, as are computers based on the Intel 80386 and higher-level microprocessors.

32-bit operating system. An operating system in which 4 bytes, or 32 bits, can be processed at one time. Windows 98, Windows XP, Windows NT, Linux, and OS/2 are examples. See also instruction set, protected mode.

386 Processor. 386 processor (or 80386 processor) was introduced in 1985, by Intel, which was the first processor to use 32-bit addressing, allowing it to utilise up to 4 Gigabytes of memory. The 386 processor was manufactured in many different versions and ran at speeds from 16 Mhz through to 40 Mhz.

Image 3: Intel 80386 processor

3-D graphic. Any graphical image that depicts one or more objects in three dimensions—height, width, and depth. A 3-D graphic is rendered on a two-dimensional medium; the third dimension, depth, is indicated by means of perspective and by techniques such as shading or gradient use of color.

3G. Acronym for 3rd Generation. The third generation of digital wireless technology, as defined by the International Telecommunications Union (ITU). Third generation technology is expected to deliver data transmission speeds between 144 Kbps (kilobits per second) and 2 Mbps (megabits per second), compared to the 9.6 Kbps to 19.2 Kbps offered by second generation technology. Western Europe and Japan lead the world in adoption of 3G technology and services.

4G. Fourth Generation of Wireless Communications (or 4G) is the name for the next generation of technology for high-speed Wireless communications that is currently in research and development stage. 4G will be designed for new data services and interactive TV through mobile network.

64-bit (Machine). In computer architecture, 64-bit describes integers, memory addresses or other data units that are, at most, 64 bits (8 octets or 8 bytes) wide, or describes CPU and ALU architectures based on registers, address buses, or data buses of that size. As of 2004, 64-bit CPUs are common in servers, and have recently been introduced to the (previously 32-bit) mainstream personal computer area in the form of the AMD64, EM64T, and PowerPC 970 (or G5) processor architectures.

64-bit operating system. An operating system in which 8 bytes, or 64 bits, can be processed at one time. For Microsoft Windows, the 64-bit operating systems are Windows XP 64-Bit Edition, Windows 7 x64, Windows 8 X64 or Windows 8.1 x64. The IBM AS/400 uses a 64-bit operating system.

802.11a (Wireless, Protocol).   802.11a is an extension to IEEE 802.11 that applies to wireless LANs and provides up to 54 Mbps in the 5GHz band. 802.11a uses an orthogonal frequency division multiplexing (OFDM) encoding scheme rather than FHSS or DSSS. 802.11a, actually newer than 802.11b, offers significantly more radio channels than the 802.11b and has a shorter range than 802.11g. It isn't compatible with 802.11b. IEEE Specification: IEEE 802.11a

802.11b (Wireless, Protocol). 802.11b, also referred to as 802.11 High Rate or Wi-Fi, is an extension to IEEE 802.11 that applies to wireless LANS and provides 11 Mbps transmission (with a fallback to 5.5, 2 and 1 Mbps) in the 2.4 GHz band. 802.11b uses only DSSS. 802.11b was a ratification to the original 802.11 standard, allowing wireless functionality comparable to Ethernet. IEEE Specification: IEEE 802.11b

A

Authentic Genuine. In the context of Social Business engagement, it is the act of being open and true to the actions and words online.

A. or a See ampere.

A Links. In Telecom, a Links, also known as SS7 access links, connect an end office or signal point to a mated pair of signal transfer points. They may also connect signal transfer points and signal control points at the regional level with the A-links assigned in a quad arrangement.

A/V. A/V (Audio Video) A combination of sound (audio) and graphics (video). Camcorders can capture A/V.

A: or a: In Windows and some other operating systems, the identifier used for the first, or primary, floppy disk drive. Unless otherwise specified by changing the CMOS startup instructions, this is the drive the operating system checks first for startup instructions.

AAA. AAA stands for Authentication, Authorization, and Accounting. The AAA framework defines a set of functionalities to provide access control to network devices, such as routers, from a centralized location in the network. See Also: Access Control; Access Control System.

AAA server. An AAA server is a server with AAA Software or applications to process user requests for access to computer/network resources and to provide authentication, authorization, and accounting (AAA) functions.

ABC. 1. Acronym for Atanasoff-Berry Computer. The first electronic digital computer, created by John Atanasoff and Clifford Berry of Iowa State University in 1942. 2. Acronym for automatic brightness control. A circuit that changes the luminance of a monitor to compensate for ambient lighting conditions. 3. An imperative language and programming environment from CWI, Netherlands. This interactive, structured, high-level language is easy to learn and use. It is not a systems-programming language, but it is good for teaching or prototyping.

ABC (software). Another Bittorrent Client (ABC) is a BitTorrent client based on BitTornado. It supports a queueing system with priority, allows global and local (per torrent) preference setting for downloading torrent, provides 3 upload options and a system named Upload Rate Manager (URM) to force torrents out of queue if there isn't a pre-set upload activity. There is also an extensive web interface in ABC, allowing for other applications to view and change torrents and preferences remotely.

ABIOS. Acronym for Advanced Basic Input/Output System. A set of input/output service routines designed to support multitasking and protected mode that were built into IBM PS/2 PCs. See also BIOS.

Absolute Path. Paths that contain a complete address that anyone could use to get to a webpage. (See also **Relative path**.)

AC voltage. Alternating current used by commercial power to transmit electricity to buildings. AC voltage is available at common electrical wall outlets, and power supplies convert AC to DC.

Accelerated Indirect GLX (Software). Accelerated Indirect GLX (AIGLX) is an open source project founded by the X.Org Foundation and the Fedora Core Linux community to allow accelerated indirect GLX rendering capabilities to X.org and DRI drivers. This allows remote X clients to get fully Hardware accelerated rendering over the GLX protocol. AIGLX is also a required component to offering good performance when using an OpenGL compositing window manager, such as Compiz or Metacity.

Accelerometer. A chip in many mobile devices used to detect the orientation of the device and change the display. A basic use is to change the display to landscape or portrait mode based on the orientation. It is often combined with a gyroscope chip.

Access. Microsoft's relational database–management software for the Windows desktop platform. Part of the family of Microsoft Office products, Access in its most recent version (Access 2013) supports Access Web Apps.

Access Control. Access Control ensures that computer, network and information resources are only granted to those users who are entitled to them. Computer Security access control includes authentication, authorization and audit. It also includes additional measures such as physical devices, including biometric scans and metal locks, hidden paths, digital signatures, encryption, social barriers, and monitoring by humans and automated systems.

Access Key. A key combination, such as ALT+F, that moves the focus to a menu, a command, or a control, without using the mouse.

Access number. The telephone number used by a subscriber to gain access to an online service.

Access Point. In a wireless LAN (local area network), a transceiver that connects the LAN to a wired network. See also wireless LAN.

Access privileges. The type of operations permitted a given user for a certain system resource on a network or a file server. A variety of operations, such as the ability to access a server, view the contents of a directory, open or transfer files, and create, modify, or delete files or directories, can be allowed or disallowed by the system administrator. Assigning access privileges to users helps the system administrator to maintain security on the system, as well as the privacy of confidential information, and to allocate system resources, such as disk space. Also called: access rights. See also file protection, file server, permission, system administrator, write access.

Access provider. See **ISP**.

Access rights. See **Access privileges**.

Access speed. See **Access time**.

Access time. The amount of time it takes for data to be delivered from memory to the processor after the address for the data has been selected. 2. The time needed for a read/write head in a disk drive to locate a track on a disk. Access time is usually measured in milliseconds and is used as a performance measure for hard disks and CD-ROM drives. See also read/write head, seek time, settling time, wait state. Compare cycle time.

Access Token. Access Token is a data structure containing the Security information for a logon session in Windows or Social Media System as Facebook. It contains the Security IDs (SIDs) for the user and all the groups the user belongs to. A copy of the access token is assigned to every process launched by the user.

Accessibility. A subset of usability that refers to a website's suitability for use by anyone, regardless of age or disability. (See also **Usability**.)

Account. 1. A record-keeping arrangement used by the vendor of an online service to identify a subscriber and to maintain a record of customer usage for billing purposes. 2. The record-keeping mechanism used by networks and multiuser operating systems for keeping track of authorized users. Network accounts are created by network administrators and are used both to validate users and to administer policies—for example, permissions—related to each user.

Account Code (Telecom). Account Code is a numeric code that must be entered to dial long distance numbers in some companies to control telephone billing. Account code can protect against telephone abuse and is a way to track calls back to the person or project originating the calls.

Account Lockout. Account lockout refers to the situation in which a user account is disabled automatically for Security reasons.

Account name. The part of an e-mail address that identifies a user or an account on an e-mail system. An e-mail address on the Internet typically consists of an account name, followed by the @ (at) symbol, a host name, and a domain name. See also account (definition 2), domain name, e-mail address.

Account Policy. Account policy refers to the policies to control and manage the Security aspects of user accounts.

Account Policy. On local area networks and multi-user operating systems, a set of rules governing whether a new user is allowed access to the system and whether an existing user's rights are expanded to include additional system resources. An account policy also generally states the rules with which the user must comply while using the system in order to maintain access privileges.

Accounting file. A file generated by a printer controller that keeps track of the number of pages printed per job as well as the user that requested the print job.

Accumulator. A register used for logic or arithmetic, usually to count items or accumulate a sum.

Accuracy. The degree to which the result of a calculation or measurement approximates the true value. Compare precision (definition 1).

ACL (Access Control List). Access Control List (ACL), also known as Access List, is a mechanism that implements access control for a system resource by listing the identities of the system entities that are permitted or denied access to the resource.

ACPI. ACPI (advanced configuration power interface) An open standard used by operating systems to change the power state of devices to conserve power.

Acrobat. A program from Adobe Systems, Inc., that converts a fully formatted document created on a Windows or Macintosh platform into a Portable Document Format (PDF) file that can be viewed on several different platforms. Acrobat enables users to send documents that contain distinctive typefaces, color, graphics, and photographs electronically to recipients, regardless of the application used to create the originals. Recipients need the Adobe Reader, which is available free, to view the files. Depending on version and platform, it also includes tools such as Distiller (which creates PDF files from PostScript files).

ACT. ACT (activity) An LED on a network interface card that indicates network activity.

Action Center. A feature in Windows 8.1 by which you can view and fix problems and run automated troubleshooters, among other things.

Action query. In Microsoft Access, a query that copies or changes data. Action queries include append, delete, make-table, and update queries. They are identified by an exclamation point (!) next to their name in the Database window.

Action Statement. See **Statement.** .

ActionScript. ActionScript is a scripting language used from Macromedia Flash. It is similar in syntax to JavaScript.

Activation. 1. Activation in Networking refers to the process of enabling a subscriber device for network access and privileges on behalf of a registered account. 2. In computer Software, activation may refer to the process of enabling a user with a valid license key the privilege to use a particular Software.

Active Cell. Also called the current cell, is the cell in a spreadsheet (such as Microsoft Excel) in which numbers or formulas can be entered. The active cell shows a thick border, and its name is at the top of the screen.

Active Directory. Active Directory is a directory service that Microsoft developed for Windows domain networks and is included in most Windows Server operating systems as a set of processes and services.

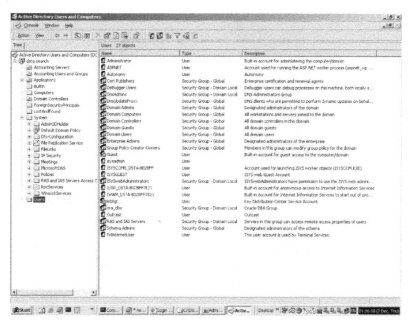

Image 4: Active Directory Users and Computers window.

Active Directory Services Interface. An administrative tool known as a Microsoft Management Console (MMC) snap-in that allows administrators to manage objects in the domain. Acronym: ADSI.

Active FTP. In networking, Active FTP is an alternative FTP mode which was designed before firewalls. In active mode FTP, the client connects from a random unprivileged port (N > 1023) to the FTP server's command port, port 21. Then, the client starts listening to port N+1 and sends the FTP command PORT N+1 to the FTP server. The server will then connect back to the client's specified data port from its local data port, which is port 20.

Active Hub. Hardware Active Hub, also known as a repeater, is a multi-ported network device that amplifies LAN transmission signals, in addition to forwarding the signals. Contrast with a passive hub, which only forwards the signals to all ports.

Active Participant. A person who sometimes comments while acquiring information and knowledge. Engagement with your participants will be based on how to pull them into more active involvement with your brand. An active participant is someone who comments, rates, or authors content in a social networking system on a regular basis.

Active partition. A partition that is bootable. On an MBR disk, one of the primary partitions is marked as active.

Active Windows. The window that is in the foreground and currently in use.

ActiveMovie. Former name for the DirectX component now known as DirectShow. Also called: DirectShow. See also **DirectX.**

ActiveSync. Is a mobile data synchronization app developed by Microsoft, originally released in 1996. It synchronizes data with handheld devices and desktop computers. In the Windows Task Manager, the associated process is called wcescomm.exe.

ActiveX. A set of technologies that enables software components to interact with one another in a networked environment, regardless of the language in which the components were created. ActiveX, which was developed by Microsoft in the mid 1990s and is currently administered by the Open Group, is built on Microsoft's Component Object Model (COM). Currently, ActiveX is used primarily to develop interactive content for the World Wide Web, although it can be used in desktop applications and other programs. ActiveX controls can be embedded in Web pages to produce animation and other multimedia effects, interactive objects, and sophisticated applications.

Activity Streams. An activity stream is a list of recent activities performed by an individual. These enable end users to blend information from internal and external sources, including blogs, wikis, business applications, and so on, so that information can be effectively used in day-to-day work and enable efficient collaboration across a broad network of people.

Actuator. Used on hard disk drive to move position read/write heads over specific tracks.

Ad Hoc. Also known as Ad hoc mode, refers to a short-term Wireless network framework created between two or more Wireless network adapters without going through an access point. In other words, an Ad hoc network allows computers to "talk" (send data) directly to and from one another. Ad hoc networks are handy for quickly trading files when you have no other way of connecting two or more computers. For an ad hoc network to work, each computer on the network needs a Wireless network card installed, and you must set your Wireless network cards (installed in each computer on the network) to Ad Hoc mode.

Ad Hoc Mode. Ad hoc mode refers to a Wireless network in which devices can communicate directly with one another without using an AP or a connection to a regular network.

Adapter Card. Or adaptor card. See Adapter.

Adapter. Or adaptor, A printed circuit board that enables a personal computer to use a peripheral device, such as a CD-ROM drive, modem, or joystick, for which it does not already have the necessary connections, ports, or circuit boards. Commonly, a single adapter card can have more than one adapter on it. Also called: interface card. See also controller, expansion board, network adapter, port1, video adapter.

Image 5: VGA Adapter Card.

Add-in. See Add-on.

Add-on. 1. A hardware device, such as an expansion board or chip, that can be added to a computer to expand its capabilities. Also called: add-in. 2. A supplemental program that can extend the capabilities of an application program. See also **Utility.**

Address. A number specifying a location in memory where data is stored. See also absolute address, address space, physical address, virtual address. 2. A name or token specifying a particular computer or site on the Internet or other network. 3. A code used to specify an e-mail destination.

Address Bar. In Internet Explorer or any web browser, the area in which you type Internet addresses, also known as URLs (uniform resource locators). Often, an Internet address takes the form of http://www.companyname.com.

Image 6: Internet Explorer Address Bar.

Address Mask. A number that, when compared by the computer with a network address number, will block out all but the necessary information. For example, in a network that uses XXX.XXX.XXX.YYY and where all computers within the network use the same first address numbers, the mask will block out XXX.XXX.XXX and use only the significant numbers in the address, YYY. See also address (definition 2).

AddThis. AddThis is a social bookmarking service that provides a code users can put on their websites so that when people visit that site, they have the option to share via Facebook, Twitter, etc. Its analytics service can show you which pages are trending, where people are interacting with your brand, and what they're saying about your content on Twitter.

Administrative Tools. A group of tools available in the Control Panel, used by administrators and advanced users.

Administrator Account. A type of Windows user account with access to all system files and settings and with permission to perform all operations. Every computer must have at least one administrator account. This account type is not recommended for daily use. See also standard user account.

Adobe Creative Cloud. Also Known as Adobe CC, is a software as a service offering from Adobe Systems that gives users access to a collection of software for graphic design, video editing, web development, photography, and cloud services. In Creative Cloud, a monthly or annual subscription service is delivered over the Internet. Previously, Adobe offered individual products as well as software suites containing several products (such as Adobe CS or Adobe eLearning Suite) with a perpetual software license. See also **Adobe Creative Suite**.

Adobe Creative Suite. Also known as Adobe CS, was a series of software suites of graphic design, video editing, and web development applications made or acquired by Adobe Systems. The collections consisted of various groupings of Adobe's applications (as Photoshop, Acrobat, InDesign, Premiere Pro, After Effects) based on various technologies (as PostScript, PDF, Flash) and organized by industry. The last version, Adobe Creative Suite 6 (CS6), was launched at a release event April 23, 2012, and released on May 7, 2012.

Adobe eLearning Suite. Adobe eLearning Suite is a collection of applications made by Adobe Systems for learning professionals, instructional designers, training managers, content developers, and educators. The suite allows users to author, manage, and publish interactive instructional information such including screencast demonstrations, simulations, and other interactive content.

Adobe Reader. A free program produced and distributed by Adobe Systems, Inc., for displaying and printing documents that are in Portable Document Format (PDF).

ADSL. ADSL (asymmetrical digital subscriber line) A specific type of DSL. ADSL uses different speeds for uploads and downloads.

Adware. Software that presents unwanted advertisements to users.

Aero Desktop. In Microsoft Windows Vista and Windows 7, Aero desktop experience features a translucent glass design with subtle window animations and new window colors. It includes distinctive visual styles that combine the appearance of lightweight, translucent windows with powerful graphic advances.

Image 7: Windows 7 desktop experience.

AES. AES (Advanced Encryption Standard) A strong encryption standard used worldwide in many applications, including with WPA2.

Affinity Analysis. A process of taking data and seeing the affinity, or relationships, of products purchases. For instance, if a person buys one product, are they more likely to buy another product? Or if they buy one product, does it make them more likely to not buy another product?

AGP. Accelerated Graphics Port (AGP), developed by Intel based on PCI, is an interface specification for the throughput demands of 3-D graphics. Rather than using the PCI bus for graphics data, AGP introduces a dedicated point-to-point channel so that the graphics controller can directly access main memory. The AGP channel is 32 bits wide and runs at 66 MHz with a total bandwidth of 266 MBps. AGP also supports two optional faster modes, with throughputs of 533 MBps and 1.07 GBps. In addition, AGP allows 3-D textures to be stored in main memory rather than video memory.

AIM. Acronym for America Online Instant Messenger. A popular instant-messaging service provided for free by America Online. With the AIM service, instant messages can be sent over an Internet connection using the AIM software or directly from a Web browser using AIM Express. See also America Online, instant messaging. Compare ICQ, .NET Messenger Service, Yahoo! Messenger.

Algorithm. An algorithm is a set of formulas developed for a computer to perform a certain function. This is important in the social sphere as the algorithms sites like Facebook and Google use are critical for developing content-sharing strategies.

Alias. 1. An alternative label for some object, such as a file or data collection. 2. A name used to direct e-mail messages to a person or group of people on a network. 3. A false signal that results from the digitization of an analog audio sample.

Alignment. The horizontal placement of a paragraph, specified by using the text-align attribute.

Allocation. In operating systems, the process of reserving memory for use by a program.

Alpha (1). Of or pertaining to software that is ready for initial testing.

Alpha (2). A software product that is under development and has enough functionality to begin testing. An alpha is usually unstable and does not have all the features or functionality that the released product is to have. Compare **Beta (2)**.

Alphanumeric. Consisting of letters or digits, or both, and sometimes including control characters, space characters, and other special characters. See also ASCII, character set, EBCDIC.

AMD (Advanced Micro Devices). One of the two primary manufacturers of CPUs. Intel is the other.

AMI BIOS. A ROM BIOS developed and marketed by American Megatrends, Inc. (AMI), for use in IBM-compatible computers. A popular feature is that its configuration software is stored in the ROM chip along with the BIOS routines, so the user does not need a separate configuration disk to modify system settings, such as amount of memory installed and number and types of disk drives. See also BIOS, Phoenix BIOS, ROM BIOS.

Ampere. The basic unit of electric current. One ampere is equivalent to a flow of 1 coulomb per second. Abbreviation: a, A, amp.

Analog. Signals that are transmitted with a sine wave. In contrast, digital data is transmitted as 1s and 0s.

Anchor. A marker within an HTML document, roughly analogous to a bookmark in a Microsoft Word document.

Android. An open source operating system used in many mobile devices. It is associated with Google but was created by a consortium of organizations. Users of Android-based devices commonly purchase applications from Google's Google Play.

Image 8: Android Logo

Antivirus software. Software used to detect, block, and remove viruses and other malware.

APIPA. APIPA (Automatic Private Internet Protocol Addressing) Address type used for DHCP clients when they don't receive a response from DHCP. An APIPA address always starts with 169.254.

APM. APM (advanced power management) An older standard used to conserve power. It has been replaced by ACPI.

App. In Windows 8 and Windows 8.1, a software program available either on the Start screen or in Apps view, which can be opened by clicking its related tile. More apps can be obtained from the Windows Store. Apps from the Windows Store are created to use the entire screen (or snapped to a portion of it) and are tailored to work well on desktop computers, laptops, tablets, and Windows Phones. Desktop apps, which are also software programs, are typically more complex and perform many functions. Desktop apps open on the desktop. Windows Store apps have fewer features than their desktop counterparts but are more streamlined and often easier to use.

Application. A program designed to assist in the performance of a specific task, such as word processing, accounting, or inventory management. Compare **Utility.** .

Application log. One of the logs in the Event Viewer. It records events from applications.

Argument. See **Attribute**.

arp. A command-line program that shows MAC-to-IP address mapping. ARP is also an acronym for Address Resolution Protocol, used to resolve IP addresses to MAC addresses. The arp command shows the result of ARP activity for a system.

ATA. ATA (advanced technology attachment) A standard for disk drive interfaces. It was derived from IDE.

ATAPI. ATAPI (advanced technology attachment packet interface) An enhancement of the ATA standard to support other drives such as CD-ROM and DVD-ROM drives.

ATM. ATM (asynchronous transfer mode) A method of transferring data over a network by using fixed-size cells instead of Ethernet packets.

Attachment. Data you add to an email, such as a photograph, a short video, a sound recording, a document, or other data. Attachments can be dangerous to open because they can contain viruses.

Attrib. Command used to view and manipulate file attributes including hidden, system, and read-only attributes.

Attribute. In HTML, text within a tag that contains information about how the tag should behave. Sometimes called argument.

ATX. ATX (Advanced Technology Extended) A common motherboard specification. ATX motherboards are 12 inches by 9.6 inches. ATX also defines power requirements associated with ATX-based power supplies.

Image 9: Connector for ATX motherboards.

AUP. Acceptable Internet Use Policy (AUP) A written agreement outlining the terms and conditions of Internet usage, including rules of online behavior and access privileges.

Authentication. Proving an identity. The three factors of authentication are something you know (such as a password), something you have (such as a smart card), or something you are (using biometrics).

Authorization. Providing access to a resource. Authenticated users are granted authorized access to resources if they have appropriate permissions.

Automatic Updates. A feature within Windows that automatically checks for updates. It can be configured to download and install updates without user intervention.

Autorun file. A file that automatically starts an installation app when you insert a disc in a drive or browse to the autorun file in a folder.

Autosense. (Or auto-negotiation) A feature on many network devices, including NICs, that automatically detects the speed and duplex mode of the connection.

Avatar. An avatar is an image or username that represents a person online within forums and social networks.

B

Back side bus. The connection between the CPU and its internal cache memory.

Background imagine. An image that displays behind the text on a webpage. By default, the image is tiled to fill the page, and scrolls with the page.

Backlight. A light used in LCD monitors to shine through LCD crystals. If the backlight fails, the LCD monitor is dim or doesn't display anything at all. Some backlights use LEDs.

Bandwidth. The transmission capacity of an electronic communications device or its rate of data transfer, usually expressed in bits per second.

Baseline. The imaginary line on which text rests.

Basic disk. The most common type of disk used in Windows-based systems. The alternative is dynamic disks.

BCC. Blind Carbon Copy. If you want to send an email to someone and you don't want other recipients to know you included that person in the email, add them to the Bcc line. BCC is like a secret copy.

BCD. See **Boot Configuration Data**.

BD-R. BD-R (Blu-ray disc Recordable) An optical Blu-ray disc that can be written to once.

BD-RE. BD-RE (Blu-ray disc Recordable Erasable) A Blu-ray disc that can be rewritten to multiple times.

Beta (1). Of or relating to software or hardware that is a beta.

Beta (2). A new software or hardware product, or one that is being updated, that is ready to be released to users for beta testing in real-world situations. Usually betas have most or all of the features and functionality implemented that the finished product is to have.

Binary. A numbering system using a base of two. It uses only 0 and 1 as valid digits.

Biometric devices. Devices that can read biometric characteristics, such as fingerprints. They are used for identification and/or authentication.

Biometrics. A method of authentication. The most common method is with fingerprints, and the strongest method is with retinal scans.

BIOS. (Basic Input/Output System) Firmware stored on a chip on the motherboard. It stores the instructions for starting the computer and includes a program used to change some settings. Current systems commonly store this on flash memory. BIOS is updated by a process called flashing.

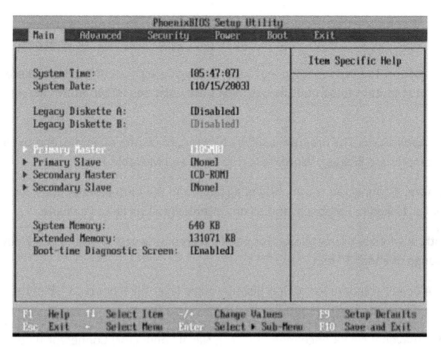

Image 10: PhoenixBIOS Setup Utility screenshot.

Bit. A single binary digit. Bits are either 0 or 1.

BitLocker Drive Encryption. BitLocker combines drive encryption and integrity checking to keep the hard disk from becoming accessed by unauthorized persons. Even if a thief steals the hard disk out of a computer and installs it in another computer, its data cannot be accessed.

Bitmap (.bmp). A patent-free digital image file format. A bitmap image consists of pixels in a grid. Each pixel is a specific color; the colors within the color palette are governed by the specific bitmap format. Common formats include monochrome bitmap, 16-color bitmap, 256-color bitmap, and 24-bit bitmap. The bitmap file format does not support transparency.

Blackout. A complete loss of power. Systems protected with an UPS will continue to run during a blackout, at least for a short period of time.

Block-level element. An element that occupies a complete paragraph or more.

Blog. A type of website used to enhance the communication and culture in a corporation or externally for marketing, branding, or public relations purposes. Blogs are online journals that you can use to share information with the rest of your organization. A blog is a great way to communicate your latest news and views in an efficient, dynamic style. By posting regular entries on a specific subject or theme, you can make sure people are kept up-to-date with the latest developments in a particular area.

Blog Host. A company that provides space on its servers to store online content such as blogs and websites. Blog hosts may be free or paid. Also called host or Web host.

Blog post editor. The section of an individual's blogging account dashboard where he or she can enter content to be published as blog posts. Also see HTML editor and visual editor.

Blogging Application. The program used by bloggers to create, maintain, and publish blogs. Examples are Blogger, WordPress, TypePad, and Movable Type.

Blogosphere. A connected community of all blogs and their interconnections, including micro-blogs, LinkedIn, Facebook, and so on. Essentially all social tools online.

Bluetooth. A wireless protocol used for personal area networks (PANs). Class 2 devices have a range of about 33 feet.

Blu-ray. A newer standard for optical discs. A single layer BD-R holds 25 GB of data, and a dual-layer disc holds 50 GB of data.

BNC. BNC (Bayonet Neill-Concelmen or British Naval Connector) Connector type used with coaxial cable.

Body. The section of an HTML document defined by the two-sided <body> tag. It contains all the information that displays in the web browser when the page is viewed.

Bold. The ability to take a risk, manage the risk, and be confident in the outcome.

Boot Configuration Data. Also Known as BCD. A file in Windows Vista–based and Windows 7–based systems in place of the Boot.ini file in Windows XP. It identifies the location of operating systems.

Boot partition. The location of the operating system files. On Windows systems this is usually C:\Windows. Compare this to the system partition that holds the boot files and is normally located at the root of the C: drive.

boot.ini. A file used in Windows XP as part of the boot process. It is not used in Windows Vista or Windows 7.

bootcfg. A command available in the Windows XP Recovery Console that can be used to rebuild the Boot.ini file.

bootrec. A command available in the Windows RE on Windows Vista and Windows 7 to repair the BCD and hard disk problems.

Botnet. Short for robot network. Group of computers, or bots, controlled by a bot herder for malicious purposes.

Brand. The tangible and intangible representation of a business or product, which includes a promise, message, and image.

Brand Advocate. A person who is passionate about your brand and references you in the normal course of business

Brand Army. A group of unpaid and paid advocates (that is, your employees!) who engage on behalf of your brand.

Brand Hijacking. Happens when consumers appropriate the brand for themselves and add meaning to it.

Breadcrumbs. A trail of hyperlinks that enable the user to back up one or more levels in the structure of a website.

Broadcast. Data sent from one computer to all other computers in the same network. The IPv4 broadcast address is 255.255.255.255.

Brownout. A temporary reduction in power. It often causes lights to flicker and can cause systems to reboot. Systems protected with an UPS are not affected by brownouts.

Browse. Browsing for a file, folder, picture, video, song, or app (among other things) is the process of navigating the operating system's folder structure to locate the desired item. Browse also describes the act of surfing the Internet.

Browser. An application used to surf the Internet. Examples are Internet Explorer, Mozilla Firefox, Opera, Safari, and Google Chrome. Also called a Web browser.

Image 11: Google Chrome Browser.

BSOD. BSOD (blue screen of death) A stop error screen that sometimes appears when a Windows-based system is unable to boot. The BSOD screen includes failure codes that indicate the source of the problem.

BTX. BTX (Balanced Technology Extended) A motherboard form factor designed by Intel as an alternative to the ATX. Intel stopped using it in 2006. ATX is the most common standard.

Burn. A term that describes the process of copying music, video, or data from a computer to a CD or DVD. The term originated because data is actually burned onto this media by using a laser. In many cases, music is burned to CDs because CDs can be played in cars and generic DVD players, and videos are burned to DVDs because videos require much more space and DVDs can be played on DVD players.

Bus. The connection between devices on a computer used to transfer data. A computer has multiple busses.

Bus topology. A logical network topology where devices are connected in a logical line. Both ends must be terminated.

Business Analytics. The discipline of turning data into insight, and using those insights to drive better business decisions.

Button-creation program. A program used to generate buttons for webpages.

Byte. A unit of measurement for data; a byte typically represents a single character, such as a letter, digit, or punctuation mark. Some single characters can take up more than one byte.

C

Cable lock. A physical lock used to secure laptops.

Cable select. A jumper selection for IDE/PATA drives. When selected for both drives, the drive connected to the black connector on the end of the ribbon cable is the master, and the drive connected to the middle gray connector is the slave.

Cable tester. A hardware tool used to test for correct wiring and possible wiring breaks within a cable.

Cache. An area used for fast access of data. CPUs use L1, L2, and sometimes L3 cache. Similarly, hard drives include RAM as cache to improve their read and write performance. Cache can also be an area on a hard drive where files are stored temporarily.

CAPTCHA. CAPTCHA (Completely Automated Public Turing Test To Tell Computers and Humans Apart) A method used to prevent webpage automated entries. Text is displayed as a distorted image that cannot be interpreted by a program. A person enters the text, proving that a person is making the entry.

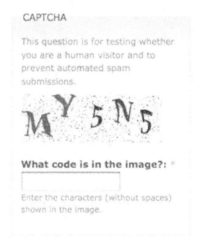

Image 12: CAPTCHA.

Cascading style sheet (CSS). A document that specifies formatting for particular tags and then can be applied to multiple webpages.

CAT. Short for category when describing twisted-pair cable types. CAT 3 can be used for 10 Mbps, CAT 5 for 100 Mbps, CAT 5e for 1 Gbps, and CAT 6 for 10 Gbps.

CC. Also known as Carbon copy. If you want to send an email to someone and you don't need that person to respond, you can put that person in the CC line. (BCC is a blind carbon copy; other recipients cannot see the BCC field address.)

CCFL. Cold Cathode Fluorescent Lamp (CCFL) A type of backlight used in LCD monitors.

CD. (compact disc) An early version of optical discs. A CD can hold up to 700 MB of data. See also CD-R and CD-ROM

cd. Command used to change a directory.

CDFS. (compact disc file system) A file system used on optical discs and widely supported by different operating systems.

CD-R. (compact disc-recordable) A CD that can be written to once. This is sometimes referred to as a WORM disc.

CD-ROM. (compact disc read-only media or compact disc read-only memory) CDs released by manufacturers that have data on them. Data can be read from these discs, but it is not possible to write to them.

Image 13: CD-ROM

CD-RW. (compact disc-rewritable) A CD that can be written to multiple times.

Cell. A distinct area of a table, into which you can place text, graphics, or even other tables.

Chain of custody. A document that tracks how evidence has been protected since the time it was collected. It helps verify that collected evidence has been controlled, preventing anyone from tampering with it.

Charging. The step in the seven-step laser imaging process where the imaging drum is charged with a high voltage. See also processing, exposing, developing, transferring, fusing, and cleaning.

Charm. The default charms are a set of five icons that appear when you swipe inward from the right side of the screen or press Windows key+C. The charms icons are Search,

Share, Start, Devices, and Settings. Apps have their own charms, generally available from the app bar found there.

Child folder. A subfolder of a parent folder.

Chipset. One or more integrated circuit (IC) chips on the motherboard that provide an interface between the CPU and the rest of the system. Compare to north bridge and south bridge.

chkdsk. A command-line tool used to check the integrity of disks. It can also fix errors and recover files.

Class. A category of content, defined by the web developer, used to apply consistent formatting among all items in that category. Similar to an ID, but multiple elements can have the same class within a document.

Classful IP address. An address with a predefined subnet mask based on the first number in the IPv4 address.

Cleaning. The step in the seven-step laser imaging process where the imaging drum is cleaned. See also processing, charging, exposing, developing, transferring, and fusing.

Click. The act of pointing to an interface element and then pressing the primary mouse button one time, usually for the purpose of selecting an item or positioning a cursor.

Closed source. Indicates that software code is not freely available. The developer views the code as a trade secret and it is not freely available. Apple's iOS is closed source.

Cloud. The cloud is a broad term that represents the Internet, specifically internet servers and data centers where data can be stored and apps can be hosted. A cloud is called a Public cloud when the services are rendered over a network that is open for public use. A personal cloud is an app of cloud computing for individuals.

Cloud Computing. A technology wherein groups of computers are connected through a network for the purpose of accessing and sharing resources that are available off premises. Cloud computing can minimize the cost that companies pay for app management and on-site hosting.

Cloud Storage. The ability to save data at an off-site location and to have it managed by a third party. In doing so, companies can save money by outsourcing data storage. Tablet, laptop, and even desktop users can store data in the cloud (rather than on their devices) and on Internet servers to make it accessible from anywhere. Microsoft SkyDrive is an example of cloud storage. You must be able to connect to the Internet to access data stored in the cloud.

Cluster. A group of sectors on a disk. Clusters are also known as allocation units. File systems use clusters to identify the location of files.

cmd. Command used to open the command prompt. See also Command Prompt.

CMOS. CMOS (complementary metal oxide semiconductor) Storage area for BIOS settings that can be changed by the user. Most current systems do not include an actual CMOS chip but instead store this information on the same flash memory where BIOS is stored.

CNR. CNR (Communications and Networking Riser) A small slot in the motherboard used for some add-on communications and networking devices such as modems or network interface cards. These features are often included in the chipset instead of by using a CNR card.

Coaxial. Cable type used in older Ethernet networks. It is similar to cable used to connect TVs to VCRs and DVD players. See RG-8 and RG-59.

Codec. Compression/decompression. A helper file that works with your media player program to play a compressed video file.

Command. An instruction you give to a computer app.

Command bar. In Internet Explorer, a toolbar located above the Content pane that provides buttons for common tasks associated with the home page, printing, web content display, and safety, as well as tools for managing Internet Explorer.

Command button. A button that executes a function.

Command Prompt. A text-based window you can use to enter MS-DOS–based commands. The application is cmd.exe, and it can be launched normally or with administrative permissions.

Communities. A group of people interacting in an online space about shared interests, topics, or material. They are not brought together because of hierarchy or authority, but rather just shared common interest. Communities provide an excellent way to connect members of a team and help them to stay in touch and share information. Communities can be public or restricted, allowing community owners to control who can join the community and access community content.

Community Manager. A person who manages an online community. This person's role is to keep the community members active and engaged by setting the strategy, gaining the trust of the members, and ensuring that the appropriate content activation plan is followed.

Compact flash. Compact flash (CF) A common type of memory used with camera and digital recorders. SD is a similar type.

Compatibility View. An Internet Explorer feature that displays a website as though you were using an earlier version of the web browser. Compatibility view was first introduced with Internet Explorer 8.

Compiled. A compiled programming language that runs the human-readable programming through a utility that converts it to an executable file (usually with an .exe or a .com extension), which is then distributed to users.

Comprehensive Analysis. A view of all that is being written about in the blogosphere about your chosen set of keywords, company, brand, or product.

Compress. To reduce the size of a set of data, such as a file or group of files, within a compressed folder that can be stored in less space or transmitted using less bandwidth.

Compressed folder. A folder containing a file or files whose contents have been compressed.

Computer Management. One of the tools in the Administrative Tools group. It includes several snap-ins, organized in three groups: System Tools, Storage, and Services And Applications.

COMx. COMx (communication port) (x=port number) A designation for a serial port, such as COM1, COM2, and so on.

Connected Standby. A new power management mode for ARM-based versions of Windows 8.1 (often installed on high-end tablet devices) that makes it possible for the device to sleep or hibernate efficiently for long periods of time. Thus, tablets and similar devices can remain turned on when not in use without draining the battery quickly.

Content Activation Strategy. A plan to create content, distribute content, promote content, and measure its success.

Content pane. In File Explorer, the pane that displays files and folders stored in the currently selected folder or storage device.

Control Panel. The window in which you can change computer settings related to system and maintenance, networks, and the Internet; user accounts; appearance; security; hardware; and sounds, among others. Control Panel opens on the desktop and is not an app.

convert. A command-line tool used to convert a FAT-based file system to NTFS without losing any data.

Cookies. Small text files that include data that identify your preferences when you visit particular websites. Cookies are generally harmless and using them makes it possible for websites such as Amazon.com to greet you by name when you navigate there.

Copy. A command that you can use to copy data to a virtual clipboard, which is a temporary holding area for data. You generally copy data so that you can paste it somewhere else.

Core. Refers to a processor within a CPU. A single CPU can have multiple cores that simulate multiple processors.

cPanel. Linux based web hosting control panel that provides a graphical interface and automation tools designed to simplify the process of hosting a web site.

Image 14: cPanel screenshot.

CPU. Central processing unit (CPU) The main circuit chip in a computer. It performs most of the calculations necessary to run the computer. Also called a processor.

Credentials. Information that provides proof of identification that is used to gain access to local and network resources. Examples of credentials are user names and passwords, smart cards, and certificates.

CRIMM. CRIMM (Continuity Rambus Inline Memory Mode) A special circuit card used with RDRAM. RDRAM must be installed in pairs, and if the second card doesn't have memory, a CRIMM is used.

Crimper. A hardware tool used to attach cables to connectors. A crimper is used to connect twisted-pair cable to RJ-45 connectors.

Crossover cable. A cable created to connect similar devices, such as a computer to a computer or a switch to a switch. Compare to a straight-through cable.

Crowdsourcing. Leveraging the wisdom of the crowd to generate new ideas and to refine ideas that exist, as well as vote on the "best" idea. Crowdsourcing leverages the collective intelligence of many people to try to solve a problem or generate new ideas. Crowdsourcing is also sometimes referred to as "wisdom of the crowd" or "collective intelligence."

CRT. CRT (cathode-ray tube) A type of display monitor. It is heavy, large, and power-hungry. CRTs have been replaced by flat panel displays in most situations.

Culture. Consists of learned ways of acting, feeling, and thinking.

Cursor. The point at which text or graphics will be inserted. The cursor usually appears on screen as a blinking vertical line, or "I-beam".

Cut. A command you use to remove the selected text, picture, or object and place it on the Clipboard. After it's pasted, the item is deleted from its original location.

D

DAC. DAC (discretionary access control) An access control model where users are owners of their files and make changes. NTFS uses the DAC model.

Daisy chain. A method of connecting devices in sequence with each other. An alternative would be having each device connect directly to a controller.

DB-25 (parallel). DB-25 (parallel communications D-shell connector, 25 pins) A D-shaped connector with 25 pins. A DB-25 port on a computer that has holes instead of pins is a parallel port.

DB-25 (serial). DB-25 (serial communications D-shell connector, 25 pins) A D-shaped connector with 25 pins. A DB-25 port on a computer that has pins instead of holes is a serial port.

DB-9. DB-9 (9-pin D shell connector) A D-shaped connector with nine pins. The DB-9 port on a computer is known as the serial port.

DC voltage. Direct current voltages supplied to electrical components. Power supplies convert AC to DC.

DDoS. DDoS (distributed denial of service) A DoS attack against a system from multiple attackers.

DDR RAM. DDR RAM (double data-rate random access memory) A shortened acronym for DDR SDRAM.

DDR SDRAM. DDR SDRAM (double data-rate synchronous dynamic random access memory) An improvement over SDRAM that doubles the clock rate by using both the leading and trailing edge of the clock. DDR2 and DDR3 are upgrades to DDR.

Default gateway. The default path out of a network for TCP/IP traffic. It is the IP address of a router's interface card on the same network as a client.

Definition list. Uses the <dl> tag; contains the complete list of headings and definition paragraphs.

Definition term. Uses the <dt> tag; a word or phrase to be defined in a definition list.

Definition description. Uses the <dd> tag; a paragraph that defines a definition term.

defrag. A command-line tool used to defragment a hard drive. It works like Disk Defragmenter.

Degaussing tool. A tool used to sanitize media. Degaussing tools have strong magnetic fields that erase data and destroy hard drives.

del. Command used to delete files in a directory.

Deprecated. A tag that should be avoided as it is in the process of being phased out or is no longer supported in the most recent version of the HTML standard.

Descriptive tag. A tag that describes the function of the text, rather than providing directions for formatting. Also called a logical tag.

Desktop. Where desktop apps run; where windows open; where you browse File Explorer; and where you work with desktop apps to write letters, create spreadsheets, manage files and folders, install and uninstall desktop apps, and do everything else you're used to doing on Windows 7, Windows Vista, and other earlier operating systems.

Desktop computer. A computer designed for use at one location. A typical desktop computer system includes the computer case containing the actual computer components, a monitor, a keyboard, a mouse, and speakers.

Desktop folder. A folder that contains icons that represent what's on your desktop. You can access this folder in File Explorer.

Details pane. In File Explorer, the pane that displays details about the selected item.

Developing. The step in the seven-step laser imaging process during which the toner is applied to the imaging drum. See also processing, charging, exposing, transferring, fusing and cleaning.

Device driver. Software that provides instructions for an operating system to use a piece of hardware.

Device Manager. A tool used to manage devices and device drivers. You can use it to disable devices and to update, uninstall, and roll back drivers.

DHCP. Dynamic Host Configuration Protocol (DHCP) server A server that manages a pool of IP addresses and client confirmation parameters and assigns IP addresses to computers and devices on a network.

Dialog box. An interface element (similar to a window) that appears on the screen, in which you can make changes to default settings in an app, make decisions when installing apps, set print options for a selected printer, configure sharing options for a file or folder, and perform similar tasks. Unlike a window, a dialog box does not include minimize and maximize buttons and you cannot resize it, but it does offer a Help button.

Digg. A social news site where content is posted by users, and the users vote on the value of the content.

Digital. Signals that are transmitted as 1s and 0s. In contrast, analog data is transmitted with a sine wave.

Digital citizen. Someone who leverages social tools in everyday use.

Digital Council. A cross-organizational body (marketing, HR, product development, supply chain, customer service, and more). In the most successful cases, it is cochaired by a line of business and IT. The mission is to explore best practices to share and replicate in the company. In addition, the Council should help craft the Social Computing Guidelines, set up a content activation strategy, create a Risk Management and Reputation Management plan, and provide guidance. It is not set up to be a blocker of social tools and techniques but rather a promoter of Social Business for competitive advantage.

Digital Immigrant. Someone who was not raised with digital tools but has adapted to them quite naturally.

Digital Native. Someone who grew up with digital tools and techniques.

Digital signature. An electronic signature that is composed of a secret code and a private key. Digital signatures are used to help verify file authenticity. Also called a digital ID.

DIMM. DIMM (dual inline memory module) A circuit card that holds RAM. Laptops use SODIMMs instead.

DIN. DIN (Deutsche Industrie Norm) The German Institute for Standardization. DIN standardized the mini-DIN connections.

DIP. DIP (dual in-line package) An integrated circuit (IC) chip. DIP chips can be plugged into DIP sockets or soldered onto a board.

dir. Command used to view a listing of files in the current directory.

Directory. MS-DOS–based name of a folder. In Windows Explorer, folders are called folders, but at the command prompt, they are called directories.

DirectX. A set of Microsoft technologies that provide developers with the tools needed to create sophisticated multimedia applications on Windows-based computers. DirectX consists of components making up two integrated layers. The Foundation layer provides low-level functions, such as support for input devices, designed to ensure that applications can run on—and take full advantage of—Windows-based hardware.

Disk Cleanup. A Windows utility that can identify and remove unneeded files on a system.

Disk Management. A GUI tool used to manage disks and volumes. Some common tasks include creating, formatting, resizing, and deleting volumes. Diskpart is a command-line equivalent.

Disk thrashing. Activity indicating that a hard drive is constantly busy. You can hear the actuator constantly seeking and see the LED constantly blinking. It can be due to a fragmented hard drive or not enough memory.

diskpart. A command-line tool that can do many of the same tasks as the Disk Management GUI.

DisplayPort. A display interface developed by VESA. The connector is rectangular with a cut-off corner.

Dithered. A color formed by a cross-hatch pattern of two colors blended together.

DLL. dynamic-link library (DLL) An operating system feature that allows executable routines (each generally serving a specific function or set of functions) to be stored separately as files with .dll extensions. These routines are loaded only when needed by the app that calls them.

DLP. DLP (Digital Light Processing) A technology used in some TVs and projectors. It is a trademark owned by Texas Instruments.

DLT. DLT (Digital Linear Tape) A self-contained tape cartridge used for backups. DLT can transfer data as fast as 60 MB/s, and 800-GB cartridges are available. It is being replaced by LTO.

DMA. DMA (direct memory access) Data transfers between memory and a device without using the CPU.

DMI. Direct Media Interface (DMI) bus. The connection between the CPU and newer chipsets instead of the front side bus.

DMZ. DMZ (demilitarized zone) A buffer zone used to protect systems that are accessible on the Internet without putting the system directly on the Internet.

DNS. Domain Name System (DNS) A technology that translates Internet address names into numerical addresses (IP addresses) so that the address can be found over the Internet. For example, if you type www.microsoft.com into a web browser, the name is translated into a numerical address and that address is used to connect you to the server hosting the Microsoft website.

Docking station. A small case into which a laptop can be plugged. It extends the capabilities of the laptop.

Domain. In Windows: A logical (rather than physical) group of resources—computers, servers, and other hardware devices—on a network, which is centrally administered through a Windows server. On the Internet: A name used as the base of website addresses and email addresses that identifies the entity owning the address.

DoS. DoS (denial of service) An attack against a system by a single attacker designed to disrupt service provided by the system. Compare with DDoS.

Double pumping. A method used to double the clock rate by using both the leading edge and trailing edge of a clock. DDR RAM types and most CPU clocks use double pumping.

Double-click. To point to an interface element and press the primary mouse button two times in rapid succession, usually for the purpose of starting an app or opening a window, folder, or file.

double-sided DIMM. Also known as double rank. Data on the DIMM is divided into two groups or ranks, and only one rank can be accessed at a time. DIMMs with chips on both sides can be single, dual, or quad rank. Compare to single-sided DIMM.

DPI. dpi (dots per inch) A printing term that identifies the resolution or clarity of the output. Higher numbers provide a higher resolution and a better-quality printout.

Drafts. A folder that holds email messages you've started and saved but not yet completed and sent.

Drag. To move an item to another location on the screen by pointing to it, holding down the primary mouse button, and then moving the mouse.

DRAM. DRAM (dynamic random access memory) A type of RAM that uses capacitors to hold data. It is cheaper than SRAM but not as fast because the capacitors need to be refreshed regularly. Compare to static RAM and synchronous dynamic RAM.

Driver. A software device driver enables Windows to communicate with a software program or hardware device (such as a printer, mouse, or keyboard) that is attached to your computer. Every device needs a driver for it to work. Many drivers, such as the keyboard driver, are built in to Windows.

DSL. DSL (digital subscriber line) A connection through a public switched telephone network (PSTN) to connect to the Internet. Asymmetric DSL (ADSL) uses different speeds for uploads and downloads. Symmetric DSL (SDSL) uses the same speed for uploads and downloads.

dual channel DRAM. RAM that is accessed in two separate 64-bit channels. It can transfer twice as much data as single channel. Compare to single channel and triple channel.

dual-boot. A system that can boot into more than one operating system. For example, a computer that can boot into Windows XP and Windows 7 is a dual-boot system.

dual-layer DVD. A DVD with 8.5 GB of storage rather than the 4.7 GB of standard DVDs. A double-sided dual-layer DVD holds 8.5 GB on each side, for a total of 17 GB.

Duplexing assembly. A component in printers that allows them to print on both sides of a sheet of paper.

DVD. DVD (digital video disc or digital versatile disc) An optical disc standard introduced after CDs. A DVD can hold 4.7 GB of data.

DVD-R. DVD-R (digital video disc-recordable) A DVD that can be written to once. This is sometimes referred to as a WORM disc.

DVD-RAM. DVD-RAM (digital video disc-random access memory) An alternative to DVD-RW. It is not widely used.

DVD-ROM. DVD-ROM (digital video disc read-only media or read-only memory) DVDs released by manufacturers that have data on them. Data can be read from these discs, but it is not possible to write to them.

DVD-RW. DVD-RW (digital video disc-rewritable) A DVD that can be written to multiple times.

DVI. DVI (digital visual interface) An interface used with displays. It includes DVI-A for analog displays, DVI-D for digital, and DVI-I integrated for both analog and digital.

dxdiag. The command that starts the DirectX Diagnostic Tool. It can diagnose problems with video and sound devices.

Dynamic disk. A special type of disk supported in Windows-based systems. Dynamic disks can be used to create striped, mirrored, and spanned volumes. The alternative is basic disks.

E

Earned. Refers to media, content, and channels that are delivered through a third party without exchange of payment. For example, in the traditional world it would be things like public relations–generated news, and analyst coverage. In the digital channel it would be things like Twitter, blogs, and product recommendations.

e-Business. A purely Internet business or part of a business that focuses on selling goods and services through the Internet

ECC. ECC (error correction code) A method used to detect and correct memory errors on high-end servers. Desktop systems typically use non-ECC RAM.

ECP. ECP (extended capabilities port) An interface used with older printers via the parallel port. It supports two way data transfers and is quicker than the plain parallel port.

EEPROM. EEPROM (electrically erasable programmable read-only memory) A chip on the motherboard used to store BIOS on older systems. It can be erased and reprogrammed with a software program by using a process commonly called flashing. Most current systems store BIOS on a type of flash memory similar to what is used with a thumb drive. See ROM, PROM, and EPROM.

EFS. EFS (encrypting file system) Part of NTFS used to scramble data. Encryption is the process of converting plain text data into cipher text data so that it cannot be read.

EIDE. EIDE (enhanced integrated drive electronics) An enhancement of the IDE standard. It is commonly referred to as PATA.

em. em A multiplier of the base font size.

EMI. EMI (electromagnetic interference) Interference from magnetic fields, such as from power cables, motors, and magnets.

EMP. EMP (electromagnetic pulse) A burst of electromagnetic radiation from an explosion. An EMP pulse can damage electronic equipment.

Engaged Clients. Clients who are attentive, interested, and active in their support for your brand, product, or company. The depth of their conversations online showcases their knowledge and care. They recommend and passionately advocate on your behalf in the blogosphere.

Engaged Employees. Those who know the company's values and are empowered to leverage those values with their partners and clients. They know their role and understand how to reach out to the right expert. These new social employees are about commitment and success.

Engagement. Your emotional connection with your client or employee, usually created by exceptional experiences that are integrated, interactive, and identifying. A Social Business connects people to expertise. It connects individuals—whether customers, partners, or employees—as networks of people to generate new sources of innovation, foster creativity, and establish greater reach and exposure to new business opportunities. It establishes a foundational level of trust across these business networks and thus a willingness to openly share information, developing a deeper sense of loyalty among customers and employees. It empowers these networks with the collaborative, gaming, and analytical tools needed to engage each other and creatively solve business challenges.

Entities. Special characters in HTML that are created by using codes beginning with ampersand (&), followed by an entity name or entity number, and then ending with a semicolon (;).

Entity name. A name that defines a special character.

Entity number. A number that defines a special character.

EPP. EPP (enhanced parallel port) An interface used with older printers via the parallel port. It is similar to ECP except that it supports direct memory access.

EPROM. EPROM (erasable programmable read-only memory) PROM that can be erased. It has a small window, and data can be erased by shining ultraviolet light into the window. The program is typically rewritten by using specialized hardware. See ROM, PROM, and EEPROM.

eSATA. eSATA (external serial ATA) An external connection for SATA devices. eSATA cables have additional shielding and can be as long as 2 meters.

eSATAp. eSATA p (external serial ATA powered) A combination of an eSATA port and a USB port that can provide power to external SATA devices. It requires a special 5-V cable to carry 5 V of power or a special 12-V cable to carry 5 V and 12 V.

ESD. ESD (electrostatic discharge) Static electricity that can build up and discharge causing damage to electronic components. Antistatic devices help prevent ESD damage.

Ethernet. A technology that uses Ethernet cables to connect computers to routers and similar hardware for the purposes of transmitting data and connecting multiple computers to form a network.

EVDO. EVDO (evolution data optimized or evolution data only) A wireless standard used with broadband Internet access.

Event Viewer. One of the tools in the Administrative Tools group. It provides access to view Windows logs, such as the Application log, the Security log, and the System log.

EVGA. EVGA (extended video graphics adapter/array) A display device resolution of 1024 × 768.

Executable file. A computer file that starts an app, such as a word processor, game, or Windows tool. You can identify executable files by their extension, .exe.

Expansion card. A circuit card that can be installed in an available expansion slot to add additional capabilities to a system. Common expansion cards use PCIe. There are many types of expansion cards, including audio cards, modems, network cards, security device cards, TV tuner cards, video cards, and video processing expansion cards.

Expert Sourcing. Leveraging the wisdom of the experts. Like crowdsourcing, but because of the level of knowledge required, experts must be used.

Explorer. Also known as Windows Explorer, used for browsing through files and folders on Windows-based systems. It is not the same as Internet Explorer.

Exposing. The step in the seven-step laser imaging process where the laser writes the image onto the imaging drum. See also processing, charging, developing, transferring, fusing, and cleaning.

ExpressCard. ExpressCard An expansion card used in laptop computers. Cards come in two versions: ExpressCard/34 and ExpressCard/54. Both can plug into the same type of ExpressCard slot.

Extended name. Another way to express color values. Extended names are similar to basic color names, but there are more of them. Not all colors named in the extended set are web-safe.

Extended partition. A partition type on basic MBR disks that supports multiple logical drives. Only one extended partition can be used on a disk. Compare to primary partition.

Extensible Markup Language. See **XML**.

External peripheral. A peripheral device installed by connecting it to a port from outside the computer. Examples are a monitor, keyboard, mouse, and speakers.

External style sheet. A plain-text file with a .css extension that defines styles to be applied to webpages.

F

FAT. FAT (File Allocation Table) A basic file system used to format disks. FAT16 (commonly called just FAT) and FAT32 are the two common versions. NTFS is recommended instead of FAT for most implementations due to better performance and security.

Favorite. A webpage for which you've created a shortcut in Internet Explorer. You can click a favorite instead of typing the web address to visit a website quickly.

Favorites bar. In Internet Explorer, a toolbar located below the Address bar that provides buttons for storing web locations for easy future access, obtaining add-ons, and accessing sites that match your browsing history.

Favorites Center. In Internet Explorer, a pane with three tabs: Favorites, on which you can save and organize links to websites and webpages; Feeds, on which you can save and organize RSS feeds; and History, on which you can view your browsing history.

F-connector. A connector used with RG-6 coaxial cable. It is commonly found on TV cable coming from a cable company.

FDD. FDD (floppy disk drive) A small disk drive that accepts 3.5-inch floppy disks. They are rarely used today.

fdisk. An old program used to partition a disk from the command prompt prior to installing an operating system.

Feed. An information stream that contains frequently updated content published by a website. Feeds are often associated with news sites and blogs but are also used for distributing other types of digital content, including photos, music, and video. See also Really Simple Syndication.

Feeder. An alternative to a paper tray used in printers. Feeders are normally on top of a printer.

Fiber. Cable type used in Ethernet networks. Data travels as light pulses along the cable. Common connectors are SC, LC, and ST.

File. A distinct piece of data. A file can be a single Microsoft Word document, a spreadsheet, a song, a movie, a picture, or even a very large single backup.

File Explorer. A window in which you can browse all the data stored on your computer and your network. You use File Explorer to access your data libraries, personal and public folders, and networked computers.

File history. The backup feature included with Windows 8.1 with which you can perform backups and, in the case of a computer failure, restore the backed-up data.

File name extension. Characters appended to the name of a file by the app that created it and separated from the file name by a period. Some file name extensions identify the app that can open the file, such as .xlsx for Microsoft Office Excel 2010 or newer files, and some represent formats that more than one app can work with, such as .jpg graphics files.

Filter. To display only items that match specified criteria.

FireWire. A standard used for high-speed serial bus transfers. FireWire 400 supports speeds of up to 400 Mbps, and FireWire 800 supports speeds of up to 800 Mbps.

FireWire port. FireWire is the brand name given to the IEEE 1394 port by Apple, Inc., one of the patent holders of IEEE 1394 technology.

Image 15: FireWire port.

Firmware. Software that is written into a hardware device. BIOS is considered firmware.

First response. Within IT, refers to actions taken by the first person that observes prohibited content or activity. Three important steps include identifying the incident, reporting the incident, and preserving data or devices from the incident.

fixboot. A command available in the Windows XP Recovery Console to fix a boot sector.

fixmbr. A command available in the Windows XP Recovery Console to fix the master boot record.

Flash drive. See **USB flash drive**.

Flashing. Process of upgrading BIOS.

Flick. To swipe a single finger quickly left, right, up, or down on a touch-enabled computer screen.

Flip. A way to move through open windows, open apps, and run apps graphically instead of clicking the item on the desktop or flicking to it. You invoke this by pressing Alt+Tab.

Fn Key. Fn key (Function key) A key used on laptop computers to provide additional uses for traditional function keys.

Folder. A data unit (similar to a folder in a filing cabinet) that holds files and subfolders. You use folders to organize data. Some folders come with Windows 8.1, including but not limited to Documents, Public Pictures, Videos, Downloads, Contacts, and Favorites.

Folder Options. A Control Panel applet used to control views in Windows Explorer.

Form data. In Internet Explorer, this is personal data, such as your name and address, that's been saved using the Internet Explorer autocomplete form data functionality. If you don't want forms to be filled out automatically, turn this feature off.

Format. Process of preparing a disk for use. Disks are formatted with a file system such as FAT32 or NTFS. Formatting an existing disk deletes the data on the disk.

FPM. FPM (fast page-mode) An early asynchronous version of DRAM. It has been replaced with synchronous versions of DRAM.

FQDN. FQDN (fully qualified domain name) A combination of a host name and a domain name. FQDNs are commonly used to address servers on the Internet.

FRU. FRU (field replaceable unit) Any component that can be replaced by a technician without returning it to a manufacturer.

FSB. FSB (front side bus) The connection between the CPU and the supporting chipset. Newer chipsets use a Direct Media Interface (DMI). Compare to back side bus.

FTP. FTP (File Transfer Protocol) Used to upload and download files to and from FTP servers. It uses port 21 and sometimes port 20. It can be encrypted with SSH.

Full-duplex. Data transmission mode specifying that data can be sent or received at the same time. Compare to simplex and half-duplex.

Function keys. Keys labeled F1 through F12 that provide shortcuts within applications. For example, F1 opens Help.

Fuser assembly. The component used in laser printers that melts the toner onto the paper.

Fusing. The step in the seven-step laser imaging process where the toner is melted onto the paper. See also processing, charging, exposing, developing, transferring, and cleaning.

Future-proofing. Ensuring that your company is anticipating the future in order to seize the opportunity that it represents.

Friend/Fan. A client or potential client who recommends your brand, company, or product because they like it so much that they feel compelled to discuss it. Someone who would recommend you, your brand, your product, or your company publicly on a social networking site

Firestorm. In social media, a firestorm is a large number of people twitting or blogging about something they have a strong opinion about. For example, in 2011, when Netflix proposed price increases, clients protested with many tweets and blogs about the issue.

Feed. A feed or news feed such as Atom or RSS allows users to subscribe to content on a web page or part of a web page.

File size. The number of bytes a file takes up on the disk.

Font family. A set of fonts listed in order of preference.

Foreground color. The default color for a webpage that can be set with the style="color: color" argument.

Frame. A section of a browser window in which a webpage loads.

Frameset. A container file that describes how many frames the browser window will be divided into and what sizes and shapes they will be.

G

Gadgets. Mini-programs that can run on the desktop of Windows 7 or in a sidebar in Windows Vista.

Game pad. A joystick replacement used with many games. It includes at least one analog stick to simulate a joystick and multiple buttons.

Image 16: GamePad

Gamification. Research into human behavior demonstrates that people are motivated by challenges that feel inherently worthwhile. Both the scholarly literature on games and the real-world experience of game designers demonstrate that people will compete for extraordinarily low-value prizes, or no prizes at all, when the experience itself is the reward. Companies and governments are beginning to use the elements of games and competitions to motivate employees, customers, and communities. This phenomenon has become known as gamification.

GB. GB (gigabyte) About 1 billion bytes; specifically, 1,073,741,824 bytes.

GDI. GDI (graphics device interface) A video card. The interface is used to send graphics to a display monitor.

Generation Y. Group of people born in the 1980s who are familiar with and in some cases, dependent upon, the Internet and electronic devices. They are sometimes called Millennials.

Geo-spatial Analysis. Part of social analytics, it enables the insight to be shaped by geographic region. For example, it could conclude that influencers are positive in London, but negative in New York City.

Geotracking. Some mobile devices record the location of the device at different times and store the information in a file on the device. Anyone who can read this file can track past locations of the device (and by implication, the owner).

Gesture. A movement you make with your finger to perform a task. Flick, swipe, tap, double-tap, and others are considered gestures. See also multitouch gesture.

GHz. GHz (gigahertz) Frequency speed commonly referring to a computer clock. One hertz (Hz) indicates that a signal can complete one cycle a second. One GHz indicates that it can complete 1 billion cycles a second.

GIF. Graphics Interchange Format (.gif) A digital image file format developed by CompuServe that is used for transmitting raster images on the Internet. An image in this format can contain up to 256 colors, including a transparent color. The size of the file depends on the number of colors used.

Globally Unique Identifier (GUID) Partition Table (GPT). Globally Unique Identifier (GUID) Partition Table (GPT) A type of disk that supports disks larger than 2 TB. Windows 7 supports up to 128 partitions on a GPT disk. Compare to MBR.

Glyph. An icon that appears on the new Windows 8.1 lock screen. You might see information about the network status, power, unread emails, and so on. You can decide which glyphs appear on the lock screen by using PC Settings.

GPS. GPS (Global Positioning System) A feature on many mobile devices that identifies the exact location of the device. Many applications use GPS, and it can be used to locate a lost device.

GPU. GPU (graphics processing unit) A processor on a video card used to create graphics. It takes the load off the CPU.

GSM. GSM (Global System for Mobile Communications) A standard used for cellular phones. GSM is incorporating 4G standards.

Guest account. A built-in Windows user account that allows limited use of the computer. When logged on to a computer with the Guest account, a user can't install software or hardware, change settings, or create a password. The Guest account is turned off (unavailable) by default; you can turn it on in the User Accounts window of Control Panel.

GUI. GUI (graphical user interface) An interface that allows users to interact by pointing and clicking rather than by using text commands.

Gyroscope. A chip in many mobile devices used to detect the orientation of the device and change the display. It is often combined with an accelerometer chip.

H

HAL. HAL (hardware abstraction layer) Part of the operating system that hides hardware differences from other parts of the operating system.

Half-duplex. Data transmission mode specifying that data can be sent or received, but not at the same time. Compare to simplex and full-duplex.

Hanging. Bullets and numbers that "hang" off the left edge of the paragraph.

Hardware. Physical computing devices that are both inside a computer and attached to it externally. Common hardware includes printers, external USB drives, network interface cards, CPUs, RAM, and more.

Hashtag. A # sign placed in a tweet to signal a topic. For instance, #ls11 was used for IBM's Lotusphere conference in 2011

HAV. HAV (Hardware Assisted Virtualization) A feature included with most CPUs to support virtualization on a system. It often has to be enabled in the BIOS.

HCL. HCL (hardware compatibility list) A list of hardware devices that have been verified to work with different versions of Windows. It is currently known as the Windows Logo'd Products List (LPL).

HDD. HDD (hard disk drive) The most common type of hard drive in computers. It includes spinning platters and read/write heads.

HDMI. HDMI (high definition media interface) A digital interface used with display monitors. It includes video and 8-channel audio.

Head. The section of an HTML document defined by the two-sided <head> tag. The Head section contains the page title and information about the document that is not displayed, such as its meta tags. It can also include lines of code that run scripts.

Header. A friendly or descriptive title that displays in the title bar of Microsoft Internet Explorer. The text is specified in a <title> tag placed in the <head> section.

Heat sink. A specially designed piece of metal that draws heat away from chips, such as the CPU. Heat sinks typically have flared fins, allowing more air through.

Hexadecimal. A numbering system using a base of 16. Valid characters are the numbers 0 through 9 and the letters A through F. A hexadecimal number can be expressed with four binary numbers.

Hibernate. A power-saving state. Data from RAM is written to the hard disk, and the system is turned off.

History. In Browsers, this is the list of websites you've visited or typed in the address bar. Anyone who has access to your computer or device and to your user account can look at your History list to see where you've been, and often it's advisable to clear your History list if you share a computer and do not have separate user accounts.

HomeGroup. A group of computers running Windows 7, Windows 8, and Windows 8.1 that have been configured to form a network. Homegroups make sharing easier because the most common sharing settings are already configured. After a homegroup is set up, you only need the proper operating system, access to the local network, and the homegroup password to join.

HomeGroup. A Windows 7 feature that allows users to easily share libraries in small networks. One user creates the homegroup and others can join it.

HomePage. The webpage that opens when you open Internet Explorer 11. You can set the home page and configure additional pages to open, as well.

Host name. A type of computer name used on networks and on the Internet. DNS resolves host names to IP addresses.

Hosted datacenter. A facility that houses and maintains computer systems, apps, resources, and associated components, such as telecommunications and storage systems. Datacenters manage the data stored there with backups, redundant power supplies, environmental controls, and so on. Hosted datacenters are in the cloud, on the Internet.

Hotspot. A wireless public network where you can connect to the Internet without being tethered to a network cable. Sometimes access to a wireless hotspot service is free, provided you have the required wireless hardware and are at a location with an open connection. You'll find wireless hotspots in libraries, coffee shops, hotels, bars, and so on.

Hot-swappable. Indicates the device can be removed without powering a system down. For example, devices connected with USB, FireWire, SATA, and eSATA connections are hot-swappable.

HTML. Hypertext Markup Language (HTML) A text markup language used to create documents for the web. HTML defines the structure and layout of a web document by using a variety of tags and attributes.

HTML. HTML (hypertext markup language) A language used to format webpages. HTML pages are retrieved from web servers by using HTTP or HTTPS.

HTML document. See **Webpage**.

HTPC. HTPC (home theater personal computer) A PC configured to work as a digital video recorder (DVR) for television, audio player for music, and video player for movies. It is often contained in a special form factor case also called HTPC.

HTTP. HTTP (Hypertext Transfer Protocol) The primary protocol used to transfer data over the web. It uses port 80.

HTTPS. HTTPS (Hypertext Transfer Protocol Secure) An encrypted version of HTTP. It uses port 443.

Hub. A device used to connect multiple devices of one type. See also **Network hub** and **USB Hub**.

Hybrid topology. A logical network topology using any two of the other types of topologies.

Hyperlink. Text or a graphic that you can click to go to a different location on a webpage, open a different webpage, start an email message, download a file, view a movie, listen to an audio clip, activate a web-based program, and more.

Hypertext Markup Language (HTML). The basic programming language of the World Wide Web.

Hypertext. See **Hyperlink**.

Hyperthreading Technology. Hyperthreading Technology (HT) An Intel technology that allows each core within a CPU to process two threads at a time. It is often combined with multiple CPUs.

HyperTransport. A technology used by AMD to increase the speed of the front side bus.

Hypervisor. Associated with virtualization, the software running on the physical host, acting as the virtual machine manager for the guest virtual machines.

I

I/O. I/O (input/output) The process of providing an input and getting an output. Many computer components provide I/O services.

ICMP. ICMP (internet control message protocol) A protocol used for diagnostics and troubleshooting. Ping and tracert commands use ICMP. ICMP traffic is often blocked by firewalls.

Icon. A visual representation of a file, folder, app, or other interface elements such as buttons that you can click or double-click as applicable, and which then opens, activates, or executes the item that the icon represents. Icon is a term generally associated with the desktop and items you find in folders, whereas tile is a term generally used to represent the items available on the Start screen.

ICR. ICR (intelligent character recognition) An advanced implementation of OCR that can read handwriting.

ID. An identifier for a unique element in a document. Similar to a class, except there can be multiple elements assigned to the same class within a document but each ID can be assigned only once per document.

IDE. IDE (integrated drive electronics) An early implementation of hard drive interfaces that moved drive controller electronics onto the drive. It was later upgraded to EIDE, standardized as ATA, and commonly referred to as PATA.

Ideation. The process of creating new ideas. It is essentially idea generation.

Identification. To personalize the experience with your clients or employees while engaging with them.

IDS. IDS (Intrusion Detection System) A system designed to monitor traffic and detect attacks.

IEEE. IEEE (Institute of Electrical and Electronics Engineers) Pronounced as "I triple E." A standards organization that has defined a wide assortment of standards for networks.

IEEE 1394a. Also known as FireWire 400. See FireWire.

IEEE 1394b. Also known as FireWire 800. See FireWire.

IIS. IIS (Internet Information Services) A web server service included in Microsoft server products.

Image. A file that contains a snapshot of all the files of a system. The image can be applied to a new computer with all of the same settings.

Image map. An overlay for a graphic that assigns hyperlinks to certain defined areas (hot spots) on the image. The hot spots can be rectangular, circular, or irregularly shaped (called a poly hot spot).

Imaging drum. A round cylinder covered with photosensitive material and used in laser printers.

IMAP. Internet Message Access Protocol (IMAP.) A method computers use to send and receive email messages. Using this protocol, you can access email without downloading it to your computer.

IMAPS. IMAPS (Internet Message Access Protocol Secure) An encrypted version of IMAP. It can be encrypted with SSL or TLS and uses port 993 by default.

Impact printer. A printer that prints by pushing print head pins against an ink ribbon pressing ink onto paper. It is commonly used to print multipart forms.

Indentation. An indentation offsets text from the usual position, either to the right or to the left. In HTML, the three types of indentation you can set are first-line indent, padding, and margin.

Information Technology. Also known as IT. The development, installation, and implementation of computer systems and apps.

Infrastructure mode. A wireless network created with a WAP or wireless router. In contrast, in ad-hoc mode devices connect to each other without a WAP or wireless router.

Inkjet printer. A color printer popular with home users that prints by injecting ink onto a piece of paper.

Inline span. A shell into which you can place any arguments you need.

InPrivate Browsing. A browsing mode that opens a separate Internet Explorer window in which the places you visit are not tracked. The pages and sites do not appear on the History tab, and temporary files and cookies are not saved on your computer.

Input device. A piece of hardware with which you type, select, open, or otherwise interact with the computer. Common input devices include the mouse and keyboard. However, your finger can be an input device, and there are several specialty input devices for people with disabilities.

Integrate. The act of having your clients or employees become active participants, not spectator.

Integrated Graphics Processing Unit. Integrated graphics processing unit (GPU) Indicates that the GPU is included either within the chipset or within the CPU. An integrated GPU is not as powerful as a dedicated graphics card.

Intel. One of the two primary manufacturers of CPUs. AMD is the other.

Interact. The act of presenting your online presence and your offline presence as a single experience.

Interface. What you see on the screen when working on a computer. In the WordPad interface, you see the ribbon, tabs, and the page itself, for instance.

Internal peripheral. A device installed inside the computer's case, such as an expansion card, a hard disk, or a DVD drive. See also external peripheral and peripheral device.

Internet. The worldwide collection of networks and gateways that use the TCP/IP suite of protocols to communicate with one another. At the heart of the Internet is a backbone of high-speed data communication lines between major nodes or host computers, consisting of thousands of commercial, government, educational, and other computer systems, that route data and messages.

Internet Explorer. Microsoft's Web browsing software. Introduced in October 1995. Internet Explorer 11 is the newest version of the Microsoft web browser. It's available as both a Windows Store–style app and a desktop app.

Internet Options. A Control Panel applet used to manipulate settings for Internet Explorer.

Internet Protocol address. An address that identifies a computer that is connected to the Internet or to a network. There are two types of IP addresses: IP version 4 (IPv4) and IP version 6 (IPv6). An IPv4 address usually consists of four groups of numbers separated by periods, such as 192.168.1.69. An IPv6 address has eight groups of hexadecimal characters (the numbers 0 through 9 and the letters a through f) separated by colons—for example, 3ffe:ffff:0000:2f3b: 02aa:00ff:fe28.1:9c5a.

Internet Protocol security. Internet Protocol security (IP sec) An encryption protocol used on internal networks and on the Internet. It is often used in virtual private network (VPN) tunnels.

Internet Server. A computer that stores data offsite, such as one that might store your email before you download it or hold backups you store in the cloud. Through Internet servers, you can access information from any computer that can access the Internet.

Interpreted. A program that is distributed in human-readable format to users, and the program in which it is opened takes care of running it.

Inverter. Used in laptop computers with LCD displays. It converts DC voltage to AC voltage for the CCFL backlight.

iOS. The primary operating system used on Applebased mobile devices. It is a closed source, vendor-specific operating system. Apple doesn't license its use on any devices other than Apple products. Users of iOS-based devices can purchase and download applications from Apple's App Store.

IP. See Internet Protocol address

ipconfig. A command-line program used to view IP configuration information on a system. It includes multiple switches, including the /release and /renew switches used to release and renew information from a DHCP server.

IR. IR (infrared) A line-of-sight wireless standard. It allows devices to transmit and receive data using LEDs and IR sensors, similarly to how TV remote controllers work.

IrDA. IrDA (Infrared Data Association) An organization that develops and maintains IR standards.

IRQ. IRQ (interrupt request) A number assigned to a device that allows it to get the attention of the CPU. IRQs are automatically assigned with plug and play.

ISA. ISA (industry standard architecture) An older expansion card standard using 8 bits or 16 bits. It was replaced with Extended ISA (EISA) and then the different PCI standards. It is not used in current systems.

ISDN. ISDN (integrated services digital network) A special type of dial-up connection to the Internet that uses a telephone network. ISDN uses terminal adapters in place of modems.

ISO. ISO (International Organization for Standardization) An international standards organization. According to the ISO, ISO is not an acronym but instead is based on the Greek word isos, meaning equal.

ISP. Internet service provider (ISP) A company that provides Internet access to individuals or companies. An ISP provides the connection information necessary for users to access the Internet through the ISP's computers. An ISP typically charges a monthly or hourly connection fee.

J

Jam. An Internet-based platform for conducting conversations through brainstorming. It connects diverse populations of individuals to gain new perspectives on problems and challenges and to develop actionable ideas centered on business-critical societal issues.

JBOD. JBOD (just a bunch of disks or just a bunch of drives) Refers to multiple disks operating independently. In some usages, it indicates a spanned volume.

JPEG. See JPG

JPG. JPG file format. A digital image file format designed for compressing either full-color or grayscale still images. It works well on photographs, naturalistic artwork, and similar material. Images saved in this format have .jpg or .jpeg file extensions.

Jump List. In Windows, an efficient method of accessing the features and files you are most likely to use with a desktop app. Right-clicking an app icon on the taskbar might offer quick access to recently opened files.

K

KB. See **Kilobyte**.

Kb. Kb (kilobit) About 1,000 bits; specifically, 1,024 bits.

Kbps. Kilobits per second; a unit of data transfer equal to 1,000 bits per second or 125 bytes per second.

Key fob. An authentication device. Key fobs display a number that is synchronized with an authentication server. Users can enter the number as a part of an authentication process.

Key Performance Indicator. Also known as KPI. A measure of performance.

Keyword. A word or phrase assigned to a file or webpage so that it can be located in searches for that word or phrase.

Kill. Unix-based command used to terminate a process.

Kilobyte. 1,024 bytes of data storage. In reference to data transfer rates, 1,000 bytes.

KVM. KVM (keyboard video mouse) A switch that allows multiple computers to share a single keyboard, video display, and monitor.

L

L1 cache. Cache used by a CPU for short-term storage of data and instructions. It is the fastest and closest to the CPU.

L2 cache. Cache used by a CPU for short-term storage of data. It is used second after L1 cache and is slower than L1.

L3 cache. Cache used by a CPU for short-term storage of data. It isn't always used, but when it is available, it is used after L1 and L2 cache.

LAN. See **Local Area Network**.

Laptop. A portable computer. Very small laptops are often called netbooks. High-performance laptops have as much power as a desktop computer.

Laser printer. A popular printer for businesses. It uses a seven-step imaging process and creates high quality outputs.

LBA. LBA (logical block addressing) A scheme used for specifying locations of blocks on a hard disk.

LC. LC (Lucent connector) Connector used with fiber cables. It was developed by Lucent Technologies and is a miniaturized version of the SC connector.

LCD. LCD (liquid crystal display) A flat panel display. It is thinner and lighter than a CRT monitor and consumes significantly less power.

LDAP. LDAP (lightweight directory access protocol) Used to access directory services databases, such as Active Directory Domain Services used in a Microsoft domain.

Leading. The amount of space between each line. Also referred to as line height..

Least privilege. Security principle that restricts access. Users are granted rights and permissions for what they need to perform their job but no more.

LED. LED (light emitting diode) A small electrical component that emits light. LEDs are commonly used on computers as indicators. For example, the power LED lights up when the computer is turned on.

LGA. land grid array (LGA) A specific type of CPU socket where the socket has pins instead of holes. The chip also has small pins created as bumps or pads. Compare to PGA.

Library (1). In Windows, a virtual data unit that previously offered access to both the related private and public folders. As an example, the Documents library offered access to the Documents and Public Documents folders, and the data was grouped to appear as a unit. In Windows 8.1, libraries only represent what is available in the related personal folder and no longer offer access to what is in the related Public folder. You can create your own libraries.

Library (2). In programming, a collection of routines stored in a file. Each set of instructions in a library has a name, and each performs a different task.

li-ion. li-ion (lithium-ion) A battery type commonly used in laptops.

Link. A shortcut to a webpage. It might be contained in an email, document, or webpage and offers access to a site without actually typing the site's name.

List item. Uses the <li> tag; an item within a numbered or bulleted list.

Loadstate. One of the two commands included with the User State Migration Tool (USMT). Loadstate loads files and settings onto a new installation. Scanstate must be run first to capture the information from the original installation.

Local Area Network. A computer network covering a small physical area such as a home or office, with a central connection point such as a network router and a shared Internet connection.

Local printer. A printer that is directly connected to one of the ports on a computer. See also remote printer.

Location-Based Service. Location-Based Service (LBS) A service that uses a GPS (global positioning system) feature of a mobile device to engage at the geographic location. It allows you to find out where your clients or friends are, to learn where their favorite places in cities or stores are, and to locate others in a common location. Common LBS services are Foursquare, Gowalla, and Jiepang.

Lock. To make your Windows computing session unavailable to other people. Locking is most effective when your user account is protected by a password.

Lock screen. A lock screen is a user interface element used by various operating systems. They regulate immediate access to a device by requiring that the user perform a certain action in order to receive access: such as entering a password, using a certain button combination, or by performing a certain gesture using a device's touchscreen.

Image 17: Lock Screen for Windows 8

Log off. To stop your computing session without affecting other users' sessions.

Log on. To start a computing session.

Logical tag. See **Descriptive tag**.

LoJack. A feature available on some laptops that can be enabled in the BIOS. It uses a transceiver that helps locate a stolen laptop similar to the way LoJack is used to recover stolen automobiles.

LOL. An acronym for laughing out loud or laugh out loud, is a common element of Internet slang

Loopback address. A predefined address used to test the functionality of TCP/IP. The IPv4 loopback address is 127.0.0.1. The IPv6 loopback address is ::1.

Loopback plug. A connector that loops output pins back to input pins. RJ-45 loopback plugs can help test NICs that have RJ-45 jacks.

LPD/LPR. LPD/LPR (line printer daemon/line printer remote) A UNIX-based protocol used to print to printers over a network.

LTO. LTO (Linear Tape-Open) A self-contained tape cartridge used for backups. LTO-5 can transfer data at 140 MB/s, and cartridges can hold as much as 1.5 TB. LTO is replacing DLT.

LVD. LVD (low voltage differential) Sometimes called LVD signaling (LVDS), a standard that transmits data as the difference in voltages between two wires in a pair. It is used by SATA, FireWire, AMDs HyperTransport, and PCIe.

M

MAC. MAC (mandatory access control) An access control model that uses labels to determine access. NTFS uses DAC instead of MAC.

Magnifier. In Windows, a tool in the Ease of Access suite of apps. You use Magnifier to increase the size of the information shown on the screen; three options are available for doing so. By default, you use your mouse to enlarge what's under it, and you can choose to what degree the material is magnified.

Mail server. A computer that your ISP configures to transmit email. It often includes a POP3 incoming mail server and an SMTP outgoing mail server. You'll need to know the names of these servers if you use an ISP to configure Microsoft Mail. Often, the server names look similar to pop.gmail.com and smtp.gmail.com.

Malware. Malicious software that includes viruses, Trojan horses, worms, and more.

MAN. MAN (metropolitan area network) Type of network that connects multiple networks together over a large metropolitan area. Worldwide Interoperability for Microwave Access (WiMAX) is used for many MANs.

MAPI. MAPI (messaging application programming interface) An interface used by application developers to create programs that can send and receive email.

Master. On PATA drives, the IDE drive that is designated as the first device. Compare to slave.

Master Boot Record. Master Boot Record (MBR) A type of disk that supports disks as large as 2 TB and up to four partitions. Compare to Globally Unique Identifier (GUID) Partition Table (GPT).

MAU. MAU (multistation access unit) A device used in ring networks. All devices communicate through the MAU but in a logical ring.

MB. See **Megabyte.**

Mb. Mb (megabit) About 1 million bits; specifically, 1,048,576 bits.

Mbps. Megabits per second; a unit of data transfer equal to 1,000 Kbps (kilobits per second).

MBR. See **Master Boot Record**.

MBSA. MBSA (Microsoft Baseline Security Analyzer) A tool available as a free download that can check one or more systems for potential security issues.

md. Command used to make a directory.

Media. Materials on which data is recorded or stored, such as CDs, DVDs, floppy disks, or USB flash drives.

Megabyte. 1,024 kilobytes or 1,048.1,576 bytes of data storage; often interpreted as approximately 1 million bytes. In reference to data transfer rates, 1,000 kilobytes.

Menu. A title on a menu bar (such as File, Edit, View). Clicking a menu name opens a drop-down list with additional choices (Open, Save, Print). Menus are being phased out by the ribbon in many apps, including those included with Windows 8.1, such as WordPad and Paint, among others.

Menu bar. A toolbar on which you can access menus of commands.

Mesh topology. A logical network topology where each device is connected to all other devices in the network.

Metadata. Descriptive information, including keywords and properties, about a file or webpage. Title, subject, author, and size are examples of a file's metadata.

Metatag. A type of header tag that provides information about the document, such as keywords.

MFD. MFD (multifunction device) Any device that performs more than one function. Multifunction printers that can print, scan, copy, and fax are common MFDs.

MFP. MFP (multifunction product) See **MFD**.

MHz. MHz (megahertz) Frequency speed commonly referring to a computer clock. One hertz (Hz) indicates that a signal can complete one cycle a second. One MHz indicates that it can complete 1 million cycles per second.

Micro-blog. A shorter form of a blog. Typically no more than 140 characters.

Micro-SD. The smallest version of SD flash card memory used in cameras and digital recorders.

Microsoft account. A sign in option by which you can synchronize settings and other data across computers, laptops, and other devices, which are applied when you log on by using the account. You need to be connected to the Internet when logging in for this to work effectively.

MIDI. MIDI (musical instrument digital interface) connector The DB-15 connection found on older sound cards for MIDI-enabled devices or joysticks. MIDI devices can play music by using .mid files, but they commonly connect with USB ports today.

MiFi. A term for wireless routers that act as mobile Wi-Fi hotspots. A MiFi device can be connected to a mobile phone carrier and provide Internet access for up to ten devices.

MIME. MIME (multipurpose internet mail extension) The standard format used to send email messages.

MIMO. MIMO (multiple-input multiple-output) Technology used by 802.11n wireless devices. They use multiple antennas to transmit and receive resulting in higher speeds.

Mini-DIN. A round connection used for many devices. The PS/2 ports are 6-pin mini-DIN ports. Other mini-DIN ports can have 3–9 pins.

Mini-SD. A smaller version of SD flash card memory used in cameras and digital recorders. It is larger than micro-SD.

Mirrored volume. See **RAID**.

MMC. MMC (Microsoft Management Console) An empty console that can be populated with snap-ins to manage Windows.

MMX. MMX (multimedia extensions) An instruction set used with Intel processors. AMD has a similar instruction set named 3DNow!

Mobile Computing. Software design and implementation tailored for mobile devices

Modem. A device through which computer information can be transmitted and received over a telephone line or through a broadband service.

Molex. A common power connector included with internal power supplies. It provides 5 V and 12 VDC to different devices, such as Parallel Advanced Technology Attachment (PATA) disk drives.

Monospace font. A font in which each letter occupies the same amount of horizontal space, regardless of its actual size and shape.

mp3. A file extension used for audio files.

mp4. A file extension used for files that include digital video with audio.

MPEG. MPEG (Moving Picture Experts Group)   A group that defines standards for audio and video compression.

msconfig. (Microsoft configuration) The command used to open the System Configuration tool. his can be used to view and manipulate what services and applications start automatically.

MSDS. (Material Safety Data Sheet) A document that identifies the contents, characteristics, and first aid responses for different materials used in a work space..

msinfo32. Command to start the System Information tool. Can be used to identify BIOS version, amount of RAM installed, processor type and speed, and much more.

mstsc. A command-line program, short for Microsoft Terminal Services Connection. It is used to open Remote Desktop Connection.

MUI. MUI (multilingual user interface) A system that can display information in different languages. When additional language files are installed, Windows can display wizards, dialog boxes, menus, and help topics in different languages.

Multiboot. Similar to dual-boot but includes systems that can boot to more than two operating systems.

Multimedia. Most often associated with video, audio, and animated images.

Multimeter. A meter that can take different types of measurements. Multimeters are commonly used to measure voltages provided by a power supply.

Multi-mode fiber. multi-mode fiber (MMF) A fiber optic cable used to transmit multiple signals at the same time. It cannot transmit signals as far as SMF can.

Multimonitor. A term used when more than one monitor is configured on a Windows computer. There are multimonitor capabilities that are new to Windows 8.1, for both the Start screen and the classic Windows desktop.

Multitouch. A feature on tablets that senses when a user touches more than one location at a time. It is commonly used for pinch and spread gestures.

Multitouch gestures. Gestures that require two (or more) fingers to perform, such as pinching the computer screen to zoom in and out.

N

NAC. NAC (network access control) A group of technologies used to inspect network clients prior to granting network access.

Narrator. A basic screen reader included with Windows 8.1 and part of the Ease of Access suite of apps. This app reads aloud text that appears on the screen while you navigate using the keyboard and mouse.

NAS. NAS (network attached storage) A dedicated computer system used to provide disk storage on a network. It's often a small device that is easy to plug in and use.

NAT. NAT (Network Address Translation) A protocol that translates private IP addresses to public and public IP addresses to private. It allows multiple internal clients to access the Internet with a single public IP address.

Native resolution. The resolution that should be used with LCD monitors. Different resolutions distort the display.

Navigate. A term used to describe surfing the Internet by browsing webpages. It is the process of moving from one webpage to another or viewing items on a single webpage. You can also navigate the data on your computer by using File Explorer.

Navigation bar. A set of hyperlinks that connect to the major pages of a website.

Navigation Pane. In Windows Explorer, the left pane of a folder window. It displays favorite links, access to SkyDrive, access to your HomeGroup, My PC, and an expandable list of storage devices and folders.

nbtstat. A command-line tool related to NetBIOS over TCP/IP Statistics. It works with NetBIOS names instead of host names.

Nested. A term referring to embedding within, as when a list is embedded within a list.

net. A command-line command. It's used for many purposes, including mapping drives with the net use command.

NET Passport. See **Windows Live ID** or **Microsoft account**.

NetBIOS. NetBIOS (Network Basic Input/Output System) name A type of computer name used on internal networks. WINS servers resolve NetBIOS names to IP addresses.

Netbook. A small, lightweight portable computer designed primarily for web browsing and simple computing. Most netbooks have limited internal resources and a screen size of less than 11 inches.

netstat. A command-line program used to view network statistics and view inbound and outbound connections.

Network. A group of computers, printers, and other devices that communicate wirelessly or through wired connections, often for the purpose of sharing both data and physical resources (such as printers). Networks often contain routers, cable modems, hubs, switches, or similar hardware to connect the computers and offer them all access to the Internet.

Network adapter. A piece of hardware that connects your computer to a network such as the Internet or a local network. Network adapters can offer wired capabilities, wireless capabilities, or both.

Network And Sharing Center. A place in Windows 8.1 where you can view your basic network information and set up connections. You can also diagnose problems here, change adapter settings, and change advanced sharing settings.

Network discovery. A feature that you must turn on so that computers can find other computers on the network. When connected to public networks, this feature is turned off by default.

Network domain. A network whose security and settings are centrally administered through a Windows server computer and user accounts.

Network drive. A shared folder or storage device on your network to which you assign a drive letter so that it appears in the My PC window as a named drive.

Network hub. A device that connects computers on a network. The computers are connected to the hub with cables. The hub sends information received from one computer to all other computers on the network.

Network printer. A printer that is connected directly to a network through a wired or wireless network connection or through a print server or printer hub.

Network profile. Information about a specific network connection, such as the network name, type, and settings.

Network router. A hardware device connecting computers on a network or connecting multiple networks (for example, connecting a LAN to an ISP).

Network share. A shared folder on a computer on your network (not your local computer).

Newsgroup. An online forum in which people participate (anonymously or not) to share ideas and opinions, get help, and meet other people with interests similar to theirs.

NIC. NIC (network interface card) Used to provide connectivity with a network. PCs commonly have built-in NICs that use an RJ-45 connector and twisted-pair cable.

NiCd. NiCd (nickel cadmium) A battery type used in older laptops.

NiMH. NiMH (nickel metal hydride) A battery type used in older laptops.

NLX. NLX (New Low-profile Extended) A motherboard form factor used by several vendors in low-profile cases. It has been superseded by Micro-ATX and Mini-ITX form factors.

NNTP. NNTP (network news transfer protocol) Used to transmit newsgroup messages between systems. Newsgroups have largely been replaced by web-based forums, so NNTP is not used often.

North bridge. Part of the CPU chipset. It provides the primary interface for high-speed devices such as the CPU, RAM, and a dedicated graphics slot and is sometimes called the memory controller hub (MCH). North bridge functions have been taken over by the CPU on newer CPUs. Compare to south bridge.

Notebook. A standard portable computer designed for all types of computing. Notebooks have technical specifications that are comparable to those of desktop computers. Most notebooks have a screen size ranging from 11 to 17 inches.

Notepad. A basic text editor. You can use it to create and modify batch files.

Notification area. The area at the right end of the Windows taskbar. It contains shortcuts to running apps and important status information.

nslookup. A command-line program used to verify the existence of records on a DNS server. It can also verify whether a DNS server can resolve a name to an IP address.

NTFS. NTFS (New Technology File System) A file system used on Windows-based systems. It is more efficient and provides much more security than do FAT-based file systems.

NTLDR. NTLDR (new technology loader) A file used in the boot process for Windows XP. NTLDR uses Boot.ini to load Windows.

NTP. NTP (Network Time Protocol) Used to synchronize computer clocks over the Internet.

O

OEM. Original equipment manufacturer (OEM.) A company that assembles a computer from components, brands the computer, and then sells the computer to the public. The OEM might also preinstall an operating system and other software on the computer.

Office 365. A product and services bundle from Microsoft that includes Microsoft Online Services as well as domain administration tools, additional account storage space, and increased vendor support.

Image 18: Office 365.

Onboard. The process of bringing a new employee into the company. See also Onboarding.

Onboarding. Onboarding refers to the mechanism through which new employees acquire the necessary knowledge, skills, and behaviors to become effective organizational members and insiders. Usually includes training, discussion of culture, and insiders.

OneDrive. Previously SkyDrive, Windows Live SkyDrive and Windows Live Folders. A location in the cloud offered by Microsoft where you can store data, including documents and pictures, among other things. Data is saved on Internet servers, and you can access the data from any Internet-enabled, compatible device.

One-sided tag. A tag that does not have a closing tag and that takes arguments.

Online. Connected to a network or to the Internet. Also used to describe time that you will be working on your computer.

On-Screen Keyboard. A feature that is available as part of Windows 8.1 with which you can input text and interact with the computer by using a virtual keyboard.

Operating System. The underlying software instructions that direct your computer what to do and how to do it. The operating system coordinates interactions among the computer system components, acts as the interface between you and your computer, makes communication possible between your computer and other computers and peripheral devices, and interacts with apps installed on your computer.

Option. One of a group of mutually exclusive values for a setting, usually in a dialog box.

Option button. A standard Windows control that you use to select one from a set of options.

Ordered list. Uses the <ol> tag; a numbered list.

Owned. Refers to media, content, and channels that the company directly delivers, has control over, or owns. For example, in the traditional world it would be things like direct mail; a call center, branch, or store; or an ATM or a kiosk. In the digital world it would be things like a blog, Facebook page, community, or microsite.

P

P2P(1). P2P People to people. The market is no longer about business-to-business (B2B) or business-to-consumer (B2C) communication, but is about people talking to people.

P2P(2). Peer-to-Peer. An Internet-based networking option in which two or more computers connect directly to each other to communicate and share files without use of a central server. Interest in P2P networking blossomed with the introduction of Napster and Gnutella.

Page title. The text in an HTML document's Head section that displays in the title bar of the web browser and on the Microsoft Windows taskbar button.

Paging file. A file stored on the hard drive that is used as virtual memory.

Paid Media. Media delivered through a third party or an intermediary in exchange for payment. For example, in the traditional world it would be things like TV, radio, or print ads. In the digital world it would be things like sponsored content or display ads.

PAN. PAN (personal area network) A network around a single person. Bluetooth is commonly used to connect mobile devices such as smartphones and ear pieces in a PAN.

Paragraph formatting. Formatting that is applicable only to entire paragraphs; it's not applied to individual characters.

Parallel. Refers to sending data as multiple bits at the same time. Before USB became popular, parallel ports were faster than serial ports.

Parent folder. A folder one level above a child folder (or subfolder).

Parity. A method used to detect errors. RAM comes in parity and non-parity versions, but desktop

Partition. A usable portion of a disk. A single physical disk can be a single partition or divided into multiple partitions. A partition is the same as a volume.

Passive Participant. Someone who uses social tools only to acquire information and knowledge. They do not comment or share their thoughts and opinions. Some articles call these folks "lurkers." They lurk around the information but do not take an active part in it.

Password. A security feature by which the user is required to input a personal password to access the computer, specific files, websites, and other data.

Password hint. An entry you record when you create or change your password to remind you what the password is. Windows displays the password hint if you enter an incorrect password.

Password reset disk. A file you create on a flash drive or other compatible media so that you can reset your password if you forget it.

Paste. A command that enables you to place previously copied or cut data in a new location. You can cut, copy, and paste a single word, sentence, paragraph, or page; a file; a folder; a web link; and more.

PATA. PATA (parallel advanced technology attachment) The common name for IDE/EIDE drives. It is being replaced by SATA.

Patch management. Practices and procedures used to keep systems up to date with current patches.

Path. A sequence of names of drives, directories, or folders, separated by backslashes (\), that leads to a specific file or folder.

PC. PC (personal computer) Any computer used by an individual.

PC Settings. A user-friendly, graphical version of Control Panel that offers access to the most-configured settings, including changing the picture on the lock screen, adding users, viewing installed devices, and configuring Windows Update.

PCI. PCI (peripheral component interconnect) An expansion card standard. It has largely been replaced by PCIe but is still used in some systems today.

PCIe. PCI e (peripheral component interconnect express) The primary expansion card standard used in systems today. It uses multiple lanes to transfer data and is identified by how many lanes it supports. A PCIe card can have 1, 2, 4, 8, 16, or 32 lanes (designated as x1, x2, x4, x8, x16, and 32).

PCI-x. PCI -x (peripheral component interconnect extended) An early enhancement for PCI primarily used on servers. Most systems use PCIe instead. PCIe and PCI-x are sometimes confused, but there are significant differences between the two.

PCL. PCL (printer control language, or printer command language) A protocol used to send print jobs to a printer.

PCMCIA. PC MCIA (Personal Computer Memory Card International Association) A standardization organization that defines standards for laptop computers. It defined the older PC Card standard and the newer ExpressCard standard.

PDA. PDA (personal data assistant) A handheld device that can include contact lists, an address book, calendar, appointment lists, and more. Many mobile devices include PDA features.

Peek. To see what's on the desktop behind currently active windows and apps. To use Peek, you position your mouse in the lower-right corner. Peek must be turned on to work.

Peer-to-Peer. See **P2P(2)**

Performance Monitor. A Control Panel applet used to measure system performance.

Peripheral. Any device that you connect to a computer. Devices can be connected using existing ports, or expansion cards can be added to provide the connectivity.

Peripheral device. A device, such as a hard disk, printer, modem, or joystick, that is connected to a computer and is controlled by the computer's microprocessor but is not necessary to the computer's operation. See also external peripheral and internal peripheral.

Permissions. Rules associated with a shared resource such as a folder, file, or printer that define who can use it and what users can do after they have access to it. You can set permissions to allow a user to print to a printer only during certain hours, for instance.

Personal folder. In Windows, a storage folder created by Windows for each user account and containing subfolders and information that is specific to the user profile, such as Documents and Pictures. The personal folder is labeled with the name used to log on to the computer.

Personalization. Personalization is about making your service targeted to the individual interests. It is based on the interests of an individual. It implies that the changes are based on implicit data, such as items purchased or pages viewed.

PGA. PGA (pin grid array) A specific type of CPU socket in which the socket has holes and the CPU has pins. Compare to LGA.

Phishing. Spam sent by attackers in an attempt to get users to click a link or provide personal information.

Photosensitive surface. A surface that reacts to light. A laser printer imaging drum uses a photosensitive surface.

Pickup rollers. Rollers in a printer used to pick up paper from a paper tray. They are used with separator pads.

Picture password. A method of logging on to windows 8 and Windows 8.1. Instead of typing a password or PIN, you can use a series of touch gestures on a particular part of an image that you select.

PII. PII (Personally Identifiable Information) Information that can be used to identify an individual. PII should be protected as sensitive data.

PIN. PIN (personal identification number) A number used for authentication. It is often combined with another method, such as with a smart card.

PIN password. A method of logging on to Windows 8 and Windows 8.1. The PIN is similar to what you type in an ATM machine and is a four-digit numeric password.

ping. A command-line program that can check network connectivity with other systems and their response times.

Pinned taskbar button. A button representing an app, which appears permanently at the left end of the taskbar. A button that is not pinned appears on the taskbar only when its app is running.

Pinning. In Windows, attaching an app, folder, or file shortcut to a user interface element such as the taskbar or Start screen.

Pixel. A pixel element. Display monitors display a pixel by using a combination of red, green, and blue dots.

PKI. PKI (public key infrastructure) A group of technologies used to create, manage, and distribute certificates. Certificates are used for several cryptographic methods, including encryption and authentication.

Platter. Used in hard disk drives. They are circular and covered in ferromagnetic material used to hold data. Hard drives typically have multiple platters.

Player. An external program that plays an audio or video file in a separate window.

Playlist. A collection of songs that you can save and then listen to as a group. You can also burn a playlist to a CD, copy a playlist to a portable music player, and more.

Plenum. Area between floors, walls, and ceilings in buildings where air is forced through for heating and cooling. Cable run through plenums must be fire-resistant and rated as plenum-safe. Non-plenum-safe cables emit toxic fumes.

Plug and Play. A technology by which the computer can automatically discover and configure settings for a device connected to the computer through a USB or IEEE 1394 connection. Also known as **PnP**.

Plug-in. A helper file that allows content that a browser does not natively support to open in a browser window.

PNG. Portable Network Graphic (.png) A digital image file format that uses lossless compression (compression that doesn't lose data) and was created as a patent-free alternative to the .gif file format.

Podcast. An online audio or video broadcast. Podcasts are generally free and can be synchronized to many types of portable music devices.

Pointer. The onscreen image that moves around the screen in conjunction with movements of the mouse. Depending on the current action, the pointer might resemble an arrow, a hand, an I-beam, or another shape.

Pointing device. A device such as a mouse that controls a pointer with which you can interact with items displayed on the screen.

POP3. A standard method that computers use to send and receive email messages. POP3 messages are typically held on an email server until you download them to your computer, and then they are deleted from the server. With other email protocols, such as IMAP, email messages are held on the server until you delete them.

POP3S. POP3S (Post Office Protocol version 3 Secure) An encrypted version of POP3. It can be encrypted with SSL or TLS and uses port 995 by default.

Pop-up. A small web browser window that opens on top of (or sometimes below) the web browser window when you display a website or click an advertising link.

Port. An interface through which data is transferred between a computer and other devices, a network, or a direct connection to another computer.

Port replicator. A connection plugged into a laptop to provide additional ports. Compare to docking station.

Portable app. Sometimes also called standalone, is a program designed to run on a compatible computer without being installed in a way that modifies the computer's configuration information. This type of application can be stored on any storage device, including internal mass storage and external storage such as USB drives and floppy disks

Portable computer. A computer, such as a notebook, laptop, or netbook, with a built-in monitor, keyboard, and pointing device, designed to be used in multiple locations.

PoS. PoS (Point of Sale) The location where a purchase is completed. Thermal printers are often used as POS locations to create receipts.

POST. POST (power-on self test) A basic test routine included in the BIOS that is run when the computer first starts. Failures are indicated by displayed errors and specific beep codes.

POST card. An expansion card that can be used to view POST cards as a system boots. They are available in PCI and PCIe versions and include an LED display to show the boot progress.

POTS. POTS (plain old telephone service) A standard telephone service available in most parts of the world. Users can use POTS and a modem for Internet access.

Power plans. A feature in Windows (Vista, 7, 8) that has configured power saving settings for hardware. The balanced plan is used for laptops when plugged in to a power source, and the power saver plan is used when laptops run on battery power.

Power supply tester. A testing device used to measure power supply voltages for power supplies that are not plugged into a motherboard.

PPM. PPM (pages per minute) A printing term that identifies the speed of a printer. Faster printers have a higher PPM.

PPP. PPP (point-to-point protocol) A protocol often used when a system connects to the Internet via an ISP.

PPTP. PPTP (point-to-point tunneling protocol) A tunneling protocol used with VPNs.

Preview pane. In File Explorer, a pane used to show a preview of a file selected in the Content pane. See also Content pane, Details pane, and Navigation pane.

Previous versions. Part of System Protection that keeps copies (previous versions) of user data. It's also called shadow copy.

PRI. PRI (primary rate interface) PRI is associated with ISDN and includes 23 64-Kbps data channels and one 16-Kbps signal channel. In North America, it's called a T1 line.

Primary display. In a multimonitor system, the monitor is specifically configured to be the main display. Most app windows appear on the primary display when they first open. See also secondary display.

Primary partition. A partition type used on disks. Basic MBR disks support up to four primary partitions, or three primary partitions and one extended partition.

Private IP address. An address assigned to a computer in a private network. Private IPv4 addresses are formally defined in the following ranges: (10.0.0.0–10.255.255.255) (172.16.0.0–172.31.255.255) (192.168.0.0–192.168.255.255)

Privileges. A combination of rights and permissions.

Processing. The step in the seven-step laser imaging process during which the raster image is processed. See also charging, exposing, developing, transferring, fusing, and cleaning.

Processor. Typically refers to the central processing unit (CPU). However, graphics cards also have a processor called the graphics processing unit (GPU).

Product key. A unique registration code issued by the manufacturer of a desktop app. The key must be supplied during the setup process to verify that you have a valid license to install and use the app.

Progress ring. The Windows 8.1 progress indicator that informs the user that a task is in progress.

Proportional font. A font in which the characters take up various amounts of space horizontally depending on their sizes.

Pseudo-class. A class that uses a variable to determine membership.

Public folder. Folders from which you can easily share data with other users. Anyone with an account on the computer can access the data here.

Q

Quick Access Toolbar. The small, thin toolbar that appears across the top of the ribbon in many apps on which you can quickly access common commands (such as Save). You can personalize this toolbar by adding your most-used commands and by repositioning it below the ribbon if desired.

Quirks mode. The mode used to process HTML pages when the browser doesn't encounter a DOCTYPE tag.

R

RAID. Originally redundant array of inexpensive disks; now commonly redundant array of independent disks. A data storage method in which data is distributed across a group of computer disk drives that function as a single storage unit. All the information stored on each of the disks is duplicated on other disks in the array. This redundancy ensures that no information will be lost if one of the disks fails. RAID is generally used on network servers where data accessibility is critical and fault tolerance is required. There are various defined levels of RAID, each offering differing trade-offs among access speed, reliability, and cost.

RAM. Random access memory. This is the hardware inside your computer that temporarily stores data the operating system or apps are using. Theoretically, the more RAM you have, the faster your computer will run. Temporary data can include a document you have written but not saved and have subsequently sent to the printer, or calculations required when resizing or otherwise editing a photo.

Reach. The number of overall friends, fans, and brand advocates you have in your domain; the number of eyeballs on your company, product, or brand

ReadyBoost. It allows any compatible mass storage device to be used as a hard-drive memory cache for the purpose of increasing random read access speed to the hard drive. Potentially compatible ReadyBoost devices include USB flash drives, flash memory, solid-state drives(SSDs), and SD cards.

Recycle Bin. The Recycle Bin holds deleted files until you manually empty it. The Recycle Bin is a safeguard that makes it possible for you to recover items you've accidentally deleted or items you thought you no longer wanted but later decide you need. Note that after you empty the Recycle Bin, the items that were in it are gone forever.

Redirect. A redirect sets up an old webpage to automatically display a new webpage.

Refresh your PC. This is a service in Windows 8.1 that, when invoked, automatically backs up all your photos, music, videos, and other personal files, reinstalls new operating system files on your computer, and then puts your data back on it for you. It also backs up and restores your customizations, changes you've made to apps, and more. By using Refresh Your PC, you can completely reinstall Windows and then easily put your data back on your computer.

Registry. A repository for information about the computer's configuration. The registry stores settings related to the hardware and software installed on the computer. Registry settings are typically updated through the proper install and uninstall procedures and apps.

Relative path. A path that defines the position of a file or folder in relation to the current location. For example, ..\Images\Picture.png defines a path up one level to the parent folder of the current location, down one level into the Images folder, to the Picture image. Relative paths are frequently used in website navigational code.

Remote Desktop Connection. An app included in Windows by which you can access your computer from somewhere else, such as an office or hotel room.

Remote printer. A printer that is not connected directly to your computer.

Reputation Management. What others believe to be true about your company, product, or brand. Reputation management is being able to appropriately shape that reputation by: Having the right listening to know what others think about you, Countering negative opinion and Building positive opinions through actions.

Reset your PC. A service in Windows 8.1 that reverts your computer to its factory settings. It does this by wiping all the data from it and reinstalling Windows, after which the computer will appear as it did the first time you turned it on, right out of the box.

Resolution. The measure of how many pixels are shown on a computer screen. A pixel is a very small square unit of display. Choosing 1024 × 768 pixels means that the desktop displays by using 1024 pixels across and 768 pixels down. When you increase the resolution, you increase the number of pixels on the screen, making images sharper yet smaller on the screen.

Restore point. A snapshot of your computer system settings taken by Windows at a scheduled time as well as before any major change, such as installing an app or updating system files. If you experience problems with your system, you can restore it to any saved restore point without undoing changes to your personal files. You use System Restore to do this.

Return on Everything. ROE Return on Everything. Return on everything that you do, including the social techniques.

Return on Investment. ROI Return on Investment. A common measure to evaluate benefits achieved versus the cost to operate.

Retweet. To take a tweet and resend it in Twitter.

Ribbon. A feature that appeared in Microsoft Office apps a few years ago and is now part of the Windows 8.1 graphical user interface. The ribbon is made up of tabs that, when selected, present a related set of tools and features. The ribbon replaces the older menu bar, menus, and drop-down menu lists.

Right-click. To point to an interface element and press the secondary (right) mouse button one time.

Rip. A term that describes the process of copying files from a physical CD to your hard disk. Generally, the term is used to describe the process of copying music CDs to the music library on your computer.

Risk Management. A plan to manage the risks of having your brand, company, or product in the blogosphere. Your brand is out there today, the major question being how to manage the brand without controlling it.

ROE. See **Return on Everything**.

ROI. See **Return on Investment**.

Router. A piece of equipment that connects two dissimilar networks and sends data from computer to computer on a LAN. A router directs the data to the correct computer and rejects data that is deemed harmful.

RSS. Really Simple Syndication (RSS.) A method of distributing information from a website or blog to subscribers for display in an RSS reader or aggregator.

Rule. An argument, especially when applied within a style tag or section.

S

Samples. A series of audio "snapshots" that are taken per second when an audio clip is digitized.

Sampling rate. The number of samples taken per second.

Screen resolution. The fineness or coarseness of detail attained by a monitor in producing an image, measured in pixels, expressed as the number of pixels wide by the number of pixels high; for example, 1024 × 768.

ScreenTip. Information that appears when you point to an item.

Scroll bar. A scroll bar appears when the content that is available to show on the screen is more than can be viewed on it. You'll see a scroll bar on the Start screen, on webpages, in long documents, and in other places.

Scrolling. A process of using the mouse, the arrow keys on a keyboard, or a flick of your finger to scroll when a scroll bar is available.

Search. A Windows 8.1 feature that that you can use to look for apps, settings, files, emails, and more. You can access Search by clicking its charm (swipe inward from the right edge of the screen or press Windows key+C), or, on the Start screen, you can simply type a description of the item for which you're searching.

Search provider. A company that provides a search engine, which you can use to find information on the Internet. For example, Google and Bing

Search term. The term you type in the Search box of the Start menu or any folder window. Windows then filters the contents of the available storage locations or of the folder window's Content pane to include only the items that contain the search term.

Secondary display. In a multimonitor system, the monitor onto which you can expand apps so that you can increase your work area. See also primary display.

Secondary tile. A special kind of Start screen tile that is created from within an app that is capable of producing one. For example, a contacts app can have its own tile, but you can also create a tile for your favorite contact on the Start screen.

Semantic tag. A tag where the name is based on its usage, such as <aside> or <article>.

Semantic zoom. The technical term for the technology by which you can pinch with two fingers to zoom in and out of the screen.

Sentiment. Understanding how people feel about your company, brand, or category based on what they write. Sentiment defines snippets of social data as positive, negative, or neutral/undefined. Social analytics turns data into insight about feelings and emotional connections.

Service Level Agreement. An agreement between your company and your friends, fans, and brand advocates on the amount of time required to respond. Commonly known as an SLA.

Share. A charm with which you can share information in one app with another app and, possibly, with other people (by Mail, for instance). This charm can also make local files or resources available to other users of the same computer or other computers on a network. You can also share items manually, such as printers and folders.

Share of Voice. Represents the percentage of the conversations for a given topic that include your brand. For example, I might have 20% share of voice for topic x (the implication being that for a given topic related to my brand, 20% of the conversations involve my brand and 80% do not).

Shared component. A component, such as a DLL file, that is used by multiple apps. When uninstalling an app that uses a shared component, Windows requests confirmation before removing the component.

Shared drive. A storage device that has been made available for other people on a network to access.

Shared folder. A folder that has been made available for other people on a network to access.

Shared printer. A printer connected to a computer and made available from that computer for use by other computers on a network.

Shortcut. An icon with an arrow on it that offers access to a particular item on the hard disk. You can put shortcuts on your desktop, for instance, that when double-clicked open apps, files, and folders stored in places other than the desktop.

Shortcut menu. A menu displayed when you right-click an object, showing a list of commands relevant to that object.

Shut down. To initiate the process that closes all your open apps and files, ends your computing session, closes network connections, stops system processes, stops the hard disk, and turns off the computer.

Shut down options. Ways in which you can disconnect from the current computing session. You can shut down the computer, switch to a different user account, log off from the computer, lock the computer, restart the computer, or put the computer into Sleep mode or Hibernate mode.

SkyDrive. Now called OneDrive. See **OneDrive**.

SmartScreen. A Windows 8.1 security technology that prevents malware from infecting your system.

SMTP. (Simple Mail Transfer Protocol) A protocol for sending messages from one computer to another on a network. This protocol is used on the Internet to route email.

Snap. The process by which you can display two to four apps side by side in Windows 8.1. This makes it possible for you to work with multiple apps at one time.

Snipping tool. A feature in Windows 8.1 by which you can drag your pointer around any area on the screen to copy and capture it. You can then save the captured data to edit it or attach it to an email or embed it in a Word document. The Snipping Tool is a desktop app.

Social Analytics. The practice of being able to understand customers and predict trends using data from the social web. Social analytics is the process of measuring, analyzing, and interpreting a brand's level of engagement, influence, sentiment, and share of voice (mindshare) across earned, paid, and owned digital channels within the context of specific business goals and objectives.

Social Analytics Manager. A person who focuses on social analytics inside of an organization. This person monitors, listens, and analyzes the sentiment (or feelings of people online), and turns the massive amounts of data into insight. This role will become increasingly important as more automated tools are coming into the market. Key skills required: Ability to understand new Social Business tools and techniques, business intelligence, and ability to make recommendations on incomplete data.

Social Bsuiness. A business that embeds "social" in all of its processes, connecting people to people, people to information, and data to insight. It is a company that engages its employees and clients in a two-way dialogue with social tools, is transparent in sharing its expertise beyond its four walls, and is nimble in its use of insight to change on a dime, It is different from social media in that social media primarily addresses or focuses on marketing and public relations. (That's where the media comes from.)

Social Business AGENDA. Social Business AGENDA A framework built from the experiences of other companies on a set of workstreams to guide the Social Business journey along: Align, Gain, Engage, Network, Design, Analyze (AGENDA).

Social Business Champion. An influential stakeholder at a company that will champion and support the use of social tools and techniques throughout the business and its processes. Usually this is the chairperson of the Digital Council.

Social Business Digital Council. A cross-organizational body (marketing, HR, product development, supply chain, customer service, and more). In the most successful cases, it is cochaired by a line of business and IT. The mission is to explore best practices to share and replicate in the company. In addition, the Council should help to craft the Social Computing Guidelines, set up a content activation strategy, create a Risk Management and Reputation Management plan, and provide guidance. It is not set up to be a blocker of social tools and techniques but rather a promoter of Social Business for competitive advantage.

Social Business Governance. The structure of relationships and processes to direct and guide the use of social techniques in order to achieve the goal of the company. The governance model defines what has to be done to reach the goals, how it is done, who has the authority to do it, and the metrics of success that will be used. Without proper governance, Social Business best practices can be implemented in departmental silos which limit the opportunity for sharing across the entire corporation.

Social Business Guidelines. A set of guidelines for employees to guide them in their use of social tools outside the firewall. Also known as Social Business Guidelines.

Social Business Manager. A person whose role it is to lead a company's transformational initiatives which empower employees to deliver business value through sharing their expertise across the social web. The Social Business manager plays an active role in the community, engaging with all audiences on an ongoing basis, working to continually grow the network and improve the experience.

Social Business Platform. The technology platform that underpins a Social Business and drives its competitiveness.

Social Business Reputation and Risk Manager. Someone whose role is to own the responsibility for listening and then filter information to the correct departments inside the organization. For example, the social reputation and risk manager may pick up a negative sentiment around supporting a product. It is not the manager's responsibility to respond, but instead it is his or her responsibility to notify the appropriate brand army (customer support and advocacy) to handle that situation.

Social Business Technologies. Extend cooperative application technologies to "socially enable" the applications and data they support. In other words, Social Business technologies are evolutionary; they integrate into the fabric of tools already in use; and they extend the ability of end users to more fully collaborate and meet objectives.

Social Capital. Connectedness of relationships people have with others, companies, and societies and the benefits these relationships bring to the individual.

Social CEO. A CEO who is active in the blogosphere. According to Forrester, by 2015, 50% of corporate boards will recruit only social CEOs.

Social Client. A client who has grown up in the digital world with gaming, mobile phones, and videos. Social clients expect customer service teams to be customer-friendly and knowledgeable about what they tweet. If your company doesn't have a great reputation, they probably won't consider your brand, and if they do decide to go with your product or offering, your teams need to be available at any time in all channels. And they expect your company to provide an experience that is like none other. On top of all that, they expect you to be able to anticipate needs before they are demanded.

Social Computing Guidelines. See **Social Business Guidelines**.

Social Curator. A person at your company who is responsible for information quality and quantity.

Social Data. Information about people (locations, relationships, expertise, etc.) that is important to engage them in appropriate networks, processes, and interactions.

Social Employee. An employee who has grown up in the digital world of gaming, mobile phones, and Facebook. Social employees expect to be social and online. And they want a leadership team that is open and involves them in the decisions.

Social Reach. Your social reach determines the number of overall friends, fans, and brand advocates you have in your domain. It is a simple measure of who is potentially listening to your subject matter expertise or expressing a belief about your company, product, or brand. Social reach is the measure of total audience (typically represented as some percentage of a total population). For example, my brand has 80% reach for males 18 to 24.

Social Techniques. A technique used to facilitate social interactions. For example, polling, jams, and discussion threads are all examples of social techniques.

Social Tool. A technology tool used by people to facilitate social interactions. For example, Facebook, Sing, MySpace, LinkedIn, and Twitter are all examples of social tools.

Social Tropes. Social ways of thinking, feeling, acting, and being.

Social Trust. Trust that is formed through online experiences and dialogues with a company, product, or brand.

Social-Enabled Process. A business process that becomes engaging and transparent through groups of people contributing and impacting the process. The collective actions of the group impact the success of the process. An example would be inserting a community voice into the product innovation process to brainstorm and refine new ideas.

Software. Apps that you use to do things with hardware, such as print to a printer. Software also refers to operating systems, desktop applications, apps, device drivers, and other computer programs that enable communications between the user and the computer hardware, most often to perform tasks.

Software piracy. The illegal reproduction and distribution of software apps.

Sound recorder. A tool included with Windows 8.1 that offers three options: Start Recording, Stop Recording, and Resume Recording. You can save recorded clips for use with other apps.

Spam. Unwanted email; junk email.

Special characters. Characters that are not included on a standard English keyboard.

Speech Recognition. An app included with Windows 8.1 by which you control your computer with your voice. Speech Recognition provides a wizard to help you set up your microphone and use the app.

Spyware. Software that can display advertisements (such as pop-up ads), collect information about you, or change settings on your computer, generally without appropriately obtaining your consent.

Standard toolbar. Toolbar that is often underneath a menu bar in apps that do not offer a ribbon, which contains icons or pictures of common commands. You might already be familiar with the graphic icons for Save, Print, Cut, Copy, Paste, Undo, and others. These toolbars are being phased out and are being replaced by the ribbon.

Standard user account. A type of Windows user account that allows the user to install software and change system settings that do not affect other users or the security of the computer. This account type is recommended for daily use.

Standards mode. The mode used to process HTML pages when the browser encounters a DOCTYPE tag.

Start button. A button now available in the lower-right corner that, when clicked, takes you to the Start screen. You can right-click this button to access a shortcut menu that offers shut down options, access to Control Panel, and more.

Start screen. The Windows 8.1 graphical user experience that offers access to Windows Store–style and desktop apps, the desktop itself, and more. You can type while on the Start screen to locate something on it or elsewhere on your computer.

Statement. The smallest executable entity within a programming language.

Status bar. A toolbar that often appears at the bottom of an app window (such as the desktop version of Internet Explorer 11) and offers information about what is happening at the moment.

Sticky Keys. A setting by which you can configure the keyboard so that you never have to press three keys at once (such as when you must press the Ctrl, Alt, and Delete keys together to access Task Manager).

Store. See **Windows Store**.

Style. A formatting rule that can be applied to an individual tag, to all instances of a certain tag within a document, or to all instances of a certain tag across a group of documents.

Subfolder. A folder within another folder. You often create subfolders to further organize data that is stored in folders.

Subject Matter Expert. Subject Matter Expert (SME) Someone whose role is knowledge leadership and understanding a subject at an expert level. This ability is viewed as extremely valuable in today's digital world.

Swarm. A term in Foursquare, a location-based service, that signifies that more than 50 people are at a location and have "checked in" with their mobile device.

Sync. To compare data in one location to the data in another. Synchronizing is the act of performing the tasks required to match up the data. When data is synchronized, the data in both places matches.

System cache. An area in the computer memory where Windows stores information it might need to access quickly for the duration of the current computing session.

System disk. The hard disk on which the operating system is installed.

System folder. A folder created on the system hard disk that contains files required by the Windows operating system.

System Restore. In windows, this features creates and stores restore points on your computer or device's hard disk. If something goes wrong, you can run System Restore and revert to a pre-problem date by selecting the desired point in time. System Restore deals with system data only, so none of your personal data will be changed when you run it.

T

Tab. In a dialog box, tabs indicate separate pages of settings within the dialog box window; the tab title indicates the nature of the group. You can display the settings by clicking the tab. In Internet Explorer, when tabbed browsing is turned on, tabs indicate separate webpages displayed within one browser window. You can display a page by clicking its tab or display a shortcut menu of options for working with a page by right-clicking its tab.

Tabbed browsing. An Internet Explorer feature with which you can open and view multiple webpages or files by displaying them on different tabs. You can easily switch among pages or files by clicking the tabs.

Table. A grid of rows and columns, the intersections of which form cells.

Tag. A keyword or term assigned to a piece of information that helps describe an item and allows it to be found again by browsing or searching.

Tag Cloud. A collection of tags that are visually displayed. The bigger and bolder the tag, the more often it is used.

Tags. Metadata included with a file, such as the date a photo was taken or the artist who sang a particular song. You can create your own tags in compatible apps and then sort data by using those tags. In HTML, tags indicate where the formatting should be applied, how the layout should display, what pictures should be placed in certain locations, and more.

Tap (touch). A gesture you perform with your finger or a pen or stylus. A tap or touch is often the equivalent of a single click with a mouse.

Task Manager. A way to access, manage, stop, or start running apps, processes, and services. You often use Task Manager to close something that has stopped working and is unresponsive, such as an app or process.

Taskbar. The bar that runs horizontally across the bottom of the Windows 8.1 desktop. It contains icons for running apps, File Explorer, and Internet Explorer, and offers the Notification area, among other things. You can access open files, folders, and apps from the taskbar, too.

Taskbar button. A button on the taskbar representing an open window, file, or app. See also pinned taskbar button.

Theme. A set of visual elements and sounds that applies a unified look to the computer user interface. A theme can include a desktop background, screen saver, window colors, and sounds. Some themes might also include icons and mouse pointers.

This PC. An entry in the Navigation pane of File Explorer that offers access to installed hard disks, CD and DVD drives, connected external drives, network locations (drives), network media servers, and similar connected media and locations.

Tiles. Graphical user interface elements on the Windows 8.1 Start screen. Some can offer live information, such as the news headlines or the number of unread emails. Tiles are said to be pinned to the Start screen.

Tipper. Someone who influences the rest of the clients and potential clients online and offline, usually about 5% to 10% of your product's or category's population.

Title bar. The horizontal area at the top of a window that displays the title of the app or file displayed in the window as well as buttons for controlling the display of the window.

Toolbar. A horizontal or vertical bar that displays buttons representing commands that you can use with the content of the current window. When more commands are available than can fit on the toolbar, a chevron (>>) appears at the right end of the toolbar; clicking the chevron displays the additional commands.

Transition. A segue you can configure to appear when moving from one picture to another in a slide show, such as fading in or out. Transitions can be applied in other places, too, such as in Microsoft PowerPoint presentations.

Transparent. Open and with a propensity to freely share skills, knowledge, and talent, and always learning. One who is transparent therefore believes that there should be no boundaries between experts inside the company and experts in the marketplace. Transparency embraces the tools and leadership models that support capturing knowledge and insight from many sources, allowing for quick sensing of changes in customer mood, employee sentiment, or process efficiencies. It utilizes analytics and social connections inside and outside the company to solve business problems and capture new business opportunities.

Trending. Predictive trends that are occurring in the blogosphere that impact your company, brand, product, or keywords. Tools help you build models to predict behavior and recommend the next best action.

Tweet. A post or status update on Twitter of 140 characters or fewer.

Twitter. A website which offers a social networking and micro-blogging service.

Two-sided tag. Tags that enclose text between their opening and closing tags.

U

UNC. Universal Naming Convention (UNC) A system for identifying the location on a network of shared resources such as computers, drives, and folders. A UNC address is in the form of \\ComputerName\SharedFolder.

Upgrade. To replace older hardware with newer hardware or an earlier version of an app with the current version.

URL. Uniform Resource Locator (URL) An address that uniquely identifies the location of a website or webpage. A URL is usually preceded by http://, as in http://www.microsoft.com. URLs are used by web browsers to locate Internet resources.

Usability. A term referring to the experience a user has when they visit a website. Qualities included in usability are ease of learning, ease of use, memorability, error-handling, and subjective satisfaction.

USB. Universal Serial Bus (USB) A connection that provides data transfer capabilities and power to a peripheral device. See also USB hub and USB port.

USB flash drive. A portable flash memory device that plugs into a computer's USB port. You can store data on a USB flash drive or, if the USB flash drive supports ReadyBoost, use all or part of the available drive space to increase the operating system speed. See also ReadyBoost.

USB Hub. A device used to connect multiple USB devices to a single USB port or to connect one or more USB devices to USB ports on multiple computers. The latter type of USB hub, called a sharing hub, operates as a switch box to give control of the hub-connected devices to one computer at a time.

USB port. A connection that provides both power and data transfer capabilities to a hardware device.

User account. On a Windows computer, a uniquely named account that allows an individual to gain access to the system and to specific resources and settings. Each user account includes a collection of information that describes the way the computer environment looks and operates for that particular user as well as a private folder not accessible by other people using the computer, in which you can store personal documents, pictures, media, and other files. See also administrator account and standard user account.

User Account Control. (UAC) A Windows security feature that allows or restricts actions by the user and the system to prevent malicious apps from damaging the computer.

User account name. A unique name identifying a user account to Windows.

User account picture. An image representing a user account. You'll see this picture on the log in screen and at the top of the Start screen, among other places.

User Experience. Software design elements that affect how a user navigates an application or a website

User Interface. (UI) The portion of an app with which a user interacts. Types of user interfaces include command-line interfaces, menu-driven interfaces, and graphical user interfaces.

Utility. A program designed to perform a particular function; the term usually refers to software that solves narrowly focused problems or those related to computer system management. See also **Application**.

V

VESA. (Video Electronics Standards Association) A standards organization that has created standards for SVGA displays and video peripherals.

Virtual. A software system that acts as if it were a hardware system. Examples are virtual folders (called libraries) and virtual printers.

Virtual Gift. An online image or picture of an object that your company or an employee might give to someone. It is not a real item or object but exists only in the virtual world.

Virtual printer. An app that "prints" content to a file rather than on paper. When viewed in the file, the content looks as it would if it were printed.

Virus. A self-replicating app that infects computers with intent to do harm. Viruses can come as an attachment in an email, from a USB stick, from a macro in an Office app, through a network connection, and even in instant messages, among other places.

Visited hyperlink. A hyperlink to a page that has already been visited.

W

Wallpaper. The picture that appears on the desktop. Windows 8.1 comes with several options, but you can use your own picture(s) or graphics if desired.

WAN. WAN (wide area network) Two or more local area networks (LANs) connected together but in different geographic locations.

WAP. Wireless Access Point (WAP) Device that acts as a bridge for wireless clients to a wired network. WAP is also an acronym for Wireless Application Protocol.

Watt. A measure of power calculated by multiplying voltage and amperage. Power supplies are rated in watts.

Web. An abbreviated way to say World Wide Web. A worldwide network consisting of millions of smaller networks that exchange data.

Web browser. An app that displays webpage content and makes it possible for you to interact with webpage content and navigate the Internet. Internet Explorer is a web browser.

Webcam. A camera attached to a computer to provide real-time video. It is often used with phone calls. Windows 8.1 comes with a camera app that should be able to find and use your camera without any setup.

Webpage. A plain text file that has been encoded using Hypertext Markup Language (HTML) so that it appears nicely formatted in a web browser.

Web-safe color. A color that exactly matches one of the colors in a standard 8-bit display.

Website. A webpage or a group of webpages that contain related information. The Microsoft website contains information about Microsoft products, for instance.

Well-known ports. Port numbers 0 to 1023 used to identify protocols and services.

WEP. WEP (Wired Equivalent Privacy) Legacy security protocol used with wireless networks. It should not be used today.

Wi-Fi. (wireless fidelity) A technology by which an electronic device can exchange data or connect to the Internet wirelessly using radio waves. Public hotspots often offer free Wi-Fi connections to the Internet.

Wiki. A collection of web pages about a particular topic. Wikis are a great way to share information centrally and encourage collaboration within your project team. Wiki members can add their own pages, and edit and comment on existing pages, thereby ensuring that information is always kept up-to-date.

WiMAX. WiMAX (Worldwide Interoperability for Microwave Access) A wireless technology used to connect metropolitan area networks (MANs). It requires line-of-sight connectivity between towers.

Window. A display rectangle used by a graphical user interface (GUI)

Windows 7 Upgrade Advisor. A free tool used to determine whether a system is compatible with Windows 7. It checks the hardware and existing applications for compatibility issues and provides a report for the user.

Windows Anytime Upgrade. A feature in Windows 7 that allows users to a purchase an upgrade to a higher edition of Windows 7. Users purchase a license key and can upgrade the system without the installation DVD. In Windows 8, the function was renamed Add features to Windows 8.

Windows Defender. A built-in tool that provides antivirus and antimalware functionality.

Windows Easy Transfer. A tool used to transfer files and settings between two computers as part of a migration. It's included in Windows 7, and free downloads are available that can be installed on Windows XP–based and Windows Vista–based systems.

Windows Firewall. If turned on, the firewall should lessen the ability of unauthorized users to access your computer or device and its data. The firewall blocks the apps that can be a threat. You can allow apps through the firewall or create exceptions if the need arises.

Windows Live ID. An older term for an email address, registered with the Windows Live ID authentication service, that identifies you to sites and services that use Windows Live ID authentication. This has been replaced with the Microsoft account.

Windows Media Center. A full-fledged media and media management desktop app. You can view and manage photos, music, videos, and even television here. This is not included with Windows 8.1 by default; it is an add-on.

Windows Memory Diagnostic. A tool in Windows Vista and Windows 7 that is used to test physical memory.

Windows RE. Windows RE (Recovery Environment) A preinstallation environment used for troubleshooting Windows.

Windows Store. The Microsoft online store for Windows 8.1 apps. There is also an XBox Music store and an XBox Video store.

Windows To Go. A way to run Windows 8.1 from a USB key rather than from a traditional hard disk. This makes it possible for you to take Windows anywhere.

Windows Update. A service provided by Microsoft to provide updates to Windows systems.

Windows XP Mode. A feature in Windows 7 that allows you to run applications from within a virtual Windows XP environment. It is useful if you want to migrate to Windows 7 but have an older legacy application that won't run on Windows 7. The legacy application can run in Windows XP Mode within Windows 7.

WINS. WINS (Windows Internet Name System) Used to resolve NetBIOS names to IP address on internal networks. In comparison, DNS is used to resolve host names on the Internet and on internal networks.

Wire strippers. A hardware tool used to strip covering off of wires.

Wireless router. A WAP with routing capabilities. Wireless routers often have other capabilities, such as DHCP, NAT, and a firewall.

Wizard. A tool that walks you through the steps necessary to accomplish a particular task.

WLAN. WLAN (wireless local area network) A local area network using wireless technologies.

Word Wide Web Consortium (W3C). The organization that oversees HTML specifications and is the governing body for most web standards.

Workgroup. A peer-to-peer computer network through which computers can share resources, such as files, printers, and Internet connections.

WORM. WORM (write-once read-many) Indicates that a disc can be written to only once. Discs designated with R (such as DVD-R) can be written to once and are sometimes referred to as WORM discs.

Worm (Malware). Malware that can travel over a network without a host file and without user interaction.

WPA/WPA2. (Wi-Fi Protected Access) Newer security protocols used with wireless networks. WPA2 is the newest and the most secure.

WPS. WPS (Wi-Fi Protected Setup) A feature with many wireless devices that allows users to configure wireless security with a push button or a PIN. When enabled, it is vulnerable to attacks using free open source software.

WUXGA. WUXGA (wide ultra extended graphics array) A display device resolution of 1920 × 1200.

X

x64. Indicates a 64-bit processor supporting a 64-bit operating system. 64-bit versions of Windows can run on x64-based systems.

x86. Indicates a 32-bit processor supporting a 32-bit operating system. On a 64-bit Windows operating system, 32-bit application files are stored in the C:\Program Files (x86) folder by default, and 64-bit program files are stored in the C:\Program Files folder by default.

xcopy. The extended copy command is used to copy files and folders. It can do everything copy can do, but it has many more capabilities.

xD. An older type of flash memory card used in some digital cameras. Newer cameras have switched to SD.

XGA. XGA (extended graphics array) A display device resolution of 1024 × 768.

XML. Extensible Markup Language (XML) A text markup language, similar to HTML, used to define the structure of data independently of its formatting so that the data can be used for multiple purposes and by multiple apps.

XPS. XML Paper Specification (XPS) A digital file format for saving documents. XPS is based on XML, preserves document formatting, and enables file sharing. XPS was developed by Microsoft but is platform-independent and royalty-free.

Y

Y2K. See Year 2000 problem.

Yahoo! Is an American multinational Internet corporation. It is globally known for its Web portal, search engine Yahoo Search, and related services, including Yahoo Directory, Yahoo Mail, Yahoo News, Yahoo Finance, Yahoo Groups, Yahoo Answers, advertising, online mapping, video sharing, fantasy sports and its social media website.

Year 2000 problem. Prior to January 1, 2000, a potential software problem stemming from the use of two digits (99) rather than four (1999) as year indicators in computer programs. Such programs assumed that 19 preceded every year value, and so could potentially fail or produce incorrect calculations by interpreting the year 2000 (00) as an earlier date than 19xx when the year rolled over into a new century. The use of two-digit year indicators was prevalent in, though not limited to, older programs that had been written when a saving of two bytes (digits) per year value was significant in terms of computer memory. Because the use of two-digit year indicators was widespread, companies, governments, and other organizations took measures on a large scale to prevent the Year 2000 problem from affecting their computing systems. In the end, however, the problem—luckily—proved largely uneventful.

YY. The form in which the year part of a date is stored in some, mostly older, computer systems. Before 2000, the possibility existed that computers that used a 2-digit date would incorrectly interpret the year 2000 (year 00) as the year 1900 and disrupt the computer's operation.

YYYY. Symbolic of providing fully distinguished dates, including 4-digit years. Using 4-digit years was an important step in many Year 2000 remediation programs—especially those focused on data.

Z

ZIF. ZIF (zero-insertion-force) A feature often used with PGA sockets to lock a CPU into place. LGA sockets often use a locking flip-top case instead.

Zip. Zip (zigzag inline package) A file extension used for compressed files and folders.

Zoom. To enlarge a selected portion of a graphical image or document to fill a window or the screen. Zooming is a feature of many programs, including drawing, word processing, and spreadsheet programs, that allows the user to select a small part of the screen, zoom it, and make changes to the enlarged portion at a finer level of detail. See also window.

www.ingramcontent.com/pod-product-compliance
Lightning Source LLC
Chambersburg PA
CBHW080557060326
40689CB00021B/4884